Do You Want to be
Published?

- Want to become one of our authors or subject matter experts?

- Do you have a manuscript you'd like to see published?

- Have an idea for a product you want to pitch?

- **Send us a message. Your budding idea might be a new bestseller!**

We publish for all services:
Army, Air Force, Navy, and Marines
Email us: admin@mentorinc.us

MENTOR MILITARY
FOR THE MILITARY PROFESSIONAL

Books, Software, Mobile Apps, and Tools to Accelerate your Military Career
Visit MentorMilitary.com

Mentor Military—Lessons Learned—Problem Solving and Critical Thinking

Printed in USA by Mentor Enterprises Inc.

PUBLISHED BY
MENTOR®
ENTERPRISES, INC.

123 Castle Dr. STE C, Madison, AL 35758

256.830.8282

admin@mentorinc.us

1st Edition, 2021

ISBN-13: 978-1-940370-36-1

The views expressed in this book are those of the author and do not reflect the official policy or position of the United States Army, Defense Department, or the United States Government.

Disclaimer

The content of this product is a compilation of information and personal experience from the author, numerous contributors, and editors.

It is possible that mistakes may be found in both content and typography.

This book should and can only be used as a **guide**. Information gleaned from this product should be modified according to existing situations by seeking guidance from competent professionals, including your chain of command, military lawyers, inspector generals, or other competent staff professionals.

No warranty is made or implied with regard to completeness and/or correctness, legal effect, or validity of this product in any state or jurisdiction. It is further understood that any person or entity that uses this product does so at their own risk with full knowledge that they have a legal obligation, duty, and responsibility to ensure the information they use or provide to others is in accordance with up-to-date military law, procedure, regulation, policy, and order. No part of this product shall in any way substitute for professional guidance or regulatory requirement.

MENTOR MILITARY
LESSONS LEARNED
PROBLEM SOLVING &
CRITICAL
THINKING

CSM (R) MARK GERECHT &
MAJ SPENCER BEATTY

Contents

Where can I find updates?

Updates and corrections can be found online:
http://asktop.net/LL-Critical
Access Code: **68SM71HF**

WHAT IS CRITICAL THINKING?

OVERUSED AND MISUNDERSTOOD

Is critical thinking overused? If you examine the world today, you will see critical thinking is not overused. Much like beautiful sunrises, there could never be too much of a good thing. Instead, it is the phrase itself that is overused. Since "critical thinking" is tossed around in the same basket as intelligence, science, problem-solving, objectivity, and just a general sense of justifying the mental high ground. Everyone has some stake in believing that critical thinking is a part of their daily life. It very well may be; but it is a politically loaded concept nonetheless and therefore admitting that you did not use critical thinking to make a significant leadership decision is almost akin to admitting that you are not a "good person."

So, let's take a step back and look at critical thinking.

First of all, it is not synonymous with intelligence. It is entirely possible to have below-average intelligence and have excellent critical thinking skills and likewise possess great intelligence and simply fly by the seat of your pants on any given decision. No one should see themselves as "an idiot" if they are willing to admit they need to know more about critical thinking.

Here is an example that lives in the same space as critical thinking: Chess Mastery. Few things are more synonymous with high intelligence than having the ability to play national championship-level chess.

So, does that mean that brilliant people can simply sit down in front of a chessboard for the first time in their life and just start busting out championship moves?

Pause right there. See what just happened? We took a common perception about chess champions and then stopped for a moment, sat back, and asked a question. That is the first step on the path of critical thinking.

In such a case, instead of just walking around with a general perception about whether we should play chess because maybe we aren't "smart enough," we are now contemplating what it really means to be a competitive player. Everyone is guilty of selling themselves short at something they could have been passionate about and perhaps change their lives for the better because of unexamined perceptions.

The author spent 20 years believing he could not write a book despite having the desire to do so. That was because "authors are just way too smart, and I'm just me." Some critical thinking in the form of the chess example changed that.

Alright, now back to the question at hand. Are chess champions simply born? Does intelligence mean you can just sit down and start playing championship chess? As you learn to play chess, you may experience loss after loss. Does that mean you aren't smart or aren't lucky enough to be born with what it takes?

The answer to all these questions is no.

Chess is a game of rules, tactics, and combinations. These need to be learned, practiced, drilled, and perfected. Some standard openings or combinations may consist of a dozen moves or more with varying combinations at each step. In time, you begin to "see 20 moves ahead," in much the same way you begin to "see what specific issues might occur in a given situation." Once a specific chess piece moves into a given situation, two experienced opponents may race through the next five moves because each already knows the drill.

Critical thinking is much the same way. It is great to be highly intelligent or above average, but specific cognitive tools or tactical combinations of thought must be learned and practiced. Suffice to say, it is okay to take a minute and look more closely at this concept without seeing any assumption about whether you are intelligent, educated, or good at what you do.

Beware, once you start down the road of applying critical thinking in your life, you may start to stray from comfortable relationships, lifelong beliefs, and your engrained processes and procedures.

IT IS ABOUT CRITICAL THINKING IN THE CONTEXT OF LEADERSHIP

There are many Critical Thinking resources out there, and this book will provide shared insights, methods, and pitfalls that you may find in other resources. What makes this book different is a focus on critical thinking as a fundamental component of leadership.

In other words, you do not need critical thinking in the way that a chess master does, nor in the way that a research scientist does. If there *are* comparisons to the critical thinking skill sets you need, it would be more akin to a criminal investigator, trial attorney, or investment strategist. You must learn to duck and weave through local politics, essential relationships, bad news phone calls, people dumping sensitive or volatile information in your ear, and the sad reality that deciding which gray area is slightly better is often the best you can do. There are differences between what right looks like from a moral framework and what right looks like from a factual framework. As a judge, you must ensure the facts are clear, but the exact pronouncement of judgment will differ depending on the individual in the spotlight.

At the end of each day and the end of a long career, you will have to find a way to sleep well even though you are the only one who understood a multitude of decisions you made. Close friends and peers will at some point shake their heads and never know why you decided one way or another in a critical moment. That is leadership.

Critical thinking is a unique skill that can help you be confident in the position you take on a specific subject. It is one of many required tools for a good night's sleep after a rough day.

LET US BE PROFESSIONALLY CYNICAL

Cynicism is perceived as a negative way to view the world at large, and that might have something to do with how the word is often defined:

A perception that others are self-interested; a distrust of sincerity or integrity.

A natural cynic might even see everyone who appears to be suffering from any number of life's pains and circumstances as being mere "fakers who want attention, money, or free sympathy to cover up something else they did."

If this describes you, then you might be more prone to critical thinking.

(*BUZZ*) Wrong Answer.

What if someone *is* sincere, genuinely selfless, or suffering? That would mean that a cynical person arrives at incorrect conclusions due to faulty perceptions that feed faulty deductions. As a result, they end up missing out on a large part of the human experience around them…not to mention any number of opportunities to grow and gain wisdom and understanding. Then again, there are plenty of times in which the cynic would be correct, or perhaps be the only one in an entire organization who turned out to be right about a situation after the truth comes out.

Incidentally, that would be called *confirmation bias,* and we will discuss more on this later. But it is sort of like a gambler who believes that they have net gains due to a couple of big wins but do not see the total of accrued losses that bury those same wins. The way you see the world is earned. There is a reason you perceive any and everything the way you do. Life has taught you a unique composite of what reality is.

Critical thinking is the key to getting it right *despite* everything else life has taught you.

So why, then, is this section called "*Let Us be Professionally Cynical*"?

So far, so good. We defined the key term in this section before as opposed to just delving in based on assumptions. Then imposed an inquiry about the relevance of that definition when compared to the examples provided. Learn by doing.

In this case, the word cynical is qualified by the word "professionally." This is a type of cynicism that is a deliberate, almost mechanical method instead of a heartfelt disposition. As a professional cynic, you will pause every time significant data, rumors, emotional expressions, trending headlines, or new problems present themselves. Life has likely built neural bridges in your mind between certain types of stimulus and immediate emotional responses.

A good example would be hearing someone say something insulting about a loved one. Reflexive actions to physical threats are intense and immediate. Then there is the minor assembly of deepest-held political and religious beliefs that interweave with your very existence. These things seem obvious, but what about more routine topics such as analyzing the results of a solution you recently recommended? The way you interact with this data will be much different than other sensitive topics. This has much to do with those bridges (or lack thereof).

Consider turning some of these bridges into draw bridges that need a deliberate mechanism to be lowered. Critical thinking will train your brain to build pauses between stimulus and emotions.

The point is that you want to get it right. As a leader, your conclusions about anything happening in your area of influence will impact those that serve with you and around you.

MOST EMOTIONS ARE THE BANE OF CRITICAL THINKING

Consider that your emotional responses are robust, especially as a leader. They will funnel adrenaline, dopamine, and any number of hormones into a situation. Think about it, though. Be specific. Think about the last time something made you angry (a news-related item or in your personal life). Chances are that any number of people could have seen what you saw and not responded with anger. In fact, they could have an opposite reaction. After all, terrible news for Team A is excellent news for Team B.

So why did *you* get angry?

Yes, it is because of your unique experiences and knowledge base with the event. In truth, any person in your exact shoes would have been angry. But can you become mad without having first decided that something *is* precisely what you think it is? Didn't you have to come to a hard conclusion about something to have a strong emotional response?

At the very least, you have had the unfortunate experience of seeing a supervisor lose their cool or get angry about a situation, and you knew that they were wrong. You saw that they were only half-informed. Then you noticed how hard it was to get them to think rationally about it even after they heard the rest of the story.

Emotions are powerful. They alter your thought processes and generate so many physiological changes in your body that can lead to chronic disease or early death. As a leader, your emotions can damage an organization in domino chains of toxicity. It is too easy to develop a negative view of an individual or a team based on one misperception. That negative view becomes prejudice, and that will reverberate into hostility and missed opportunities.

What is more, look again at the inevitable fact that you must come to some sort of conclusion to provoke an emotion. This means that your mind has been made up and flash welded by hormones and feelings. You are no longer in investigate and acquire information mode. You are now officially in "you have to change my mind" mode. That is quite a different place to be when you are just starting to navigate a situation. It is the bane of critical thinking.

There is a reason why Sherlock Holmes, Hercule Poirot, Miss Marple, and Spock of Star Trek fame are known for a blank, stoic, calm demeanor except in the most extraordinary of circumstances. A great mind is a clear and deliberate mind. But then again, notice when these famous characters do take action or combine action with emotion. They act with a depth of resolve that brings all their strength and courage to the task at hand. Certainty creates boldness which marks great leaders. Critical thinking is essential for such confidence.

Your emotions are powerful, and any situation must *earn* them.

BRINGING THINGS TOGETHER

Earlier in this chapter, there was a reference to your ability to "see 20 moves ahead," in much the same way you begin to "see which specific issues might occur in a given situation."

Perhaps it already occurred to you, but that perspective, despite being earned and validated by experience, is also a preconceived idea about the situation. Such a preconception can lead to getting it wrong. Here is a scenario that brings the ideas presented thus far together in a way that most leaders have lived through in one way or another.

Let's just say "Murphy" is at it again!

You are asleep. Dead asleep. It was another one of those days where you did not get home until after 9pm. If all goes well, this much-needed rest will still only be a cat nap because you need to start your morning at 5am. Unfortunately, your phone rings at midnight, and your supervisor starts talking to you about a proposal that includes one of your team members named "Murphy."

You feel your face flush, and *now* you are awake. You tell the supervisor, "Yeah, I got it. I'll be there in 20 minutes." But you already *know* the details. Right? Same ole nonsense - different day.

Your spouse wakes up and asks if everything is okay as you cuss under your breath and start getting dressed in exaggerated lifts and tugs.

"Oh," you mutter out loud, "Just the same ole Murphy crap again."

They secretly roll their eyes, wish you good luck, and go back to sleep. But not before they hear you say, "But at least this will be the last time. Now I can get rid of that clown. The last strike means you're out!"

Now you get in your car, slam the door closed, and grip the wheel while running through all the things you will say and do in the next 12 hours to deal with Murphy by the book. As you get closer to the company, you get more and more anxious to get the dirt on the latest situation and put separation plan into action.

You don't notice, but you have been driving faster as you get closer. However, the police noticed. You pull over, and now your heart is pounding and all the tremendous adverse stress effects and swirling in your blood and stomach. You put on a good show for the officer and thank goodness it was just a warning. But maybe that was the boss that drove by while you were pulled over. Hard to tell in the dark.

You pull into the company at a 1am on the "ready to let them all have it" scale but do your best not to show your genuine emotions and take some comfort in knowing that at least the one of your team members has already begun corrective action. At least it is not a capital crime this time.

Walking into the company, you see three teammates waiting outside your office. They all appear to be upset and understand who is to blame once again. Murphy's part in this mix causes your emotional dam to crack just a little, and you blurt out some sharp crack that borders on unprofessionalism. It somehow doesn't surprise you that one of the teammates is Murphy's buddy.

Fortunately, you bring the key players into your office for the rest of the story instead of just calling Murphy in and going straight into verbal reprimands.

It turns out Murphy did the right thing. The other two teammates were having issues with each other due to some disagreements over courses of action and one of them acted without approval. Ultimately Murphy was the difference between a total screw up and a minor late-night fix. It turns out he was even ready to take total responsibility.

You sit back in your chair, let out a cleansing breath, and as the adrenaline backs off, you suddenly feel exhausted. You still have quite a situation to deal with, but much different than what you thought. You swallow your pride and calmly ask Murphy to step in.

So, let's recap. You jumped to conclusions based on your experience with Murphy and cut the messenger off short when you answered your phone. Your spouse got another glimpse of your "good side" and then incurred possible fines and embarrassment on the way to the company. It could just as well have been an accident due to emotional driving. Then there is the stress you put on your body and the fact that you broke your professional demeanor in front of your teammate. And what good did any of it do you?

That is the power of those bridges that connect certain types of stimuli directly to your emotions. No matter how you look at the situation, it is evident that critical thinking did not show up for duty till it was too late.

What would the intervention of Critical Thinking look like in this situation? As will be expounded on later, the first step is not so much a flow chart of critical thinking and problem-solving steps, but instead, self-awareness.

SELF-AWARENESS + MITIGATION = CLEAR THINKING.

Look at the issue with Murphy. Clearly, this is an individual that was getting on your hypothetical last nerve. In reality, everyone has a Murphy in their life or several Murphy's. Murphy does not have to be a person; it can be a new policy issue or a weekly requirement that drains you and your team of time and resources. Either way, there are things that are waiting to separate you from any hope of objective, critical thought, and they will rear their ugly heads at the worst possible moment.

Ideally, the reaction to the midnight phone call would have begun days or weeks before it happened. You would have recognized somewhere between Murphy's first and second strikes that you developed a physical reaction to the mention of Murphy's name. Maybe it was just a grimace or a change of tone during the weekly meetings. Perhaps you noticed that you were paying more attention to finding that third strike than on Murphy than you spent on other teammates or issues.

Whatever the "a-ha moment" is, you take control and take responsibility for this triggering mechanism in your life. The good news is that you have plenty of practice and already know how to turn these bridges into drawbridges. How so?

How about this. When you were a child, did you ever have a heated moment with a friend or a sibling, and then as soon as one of you spotted a "grown-up," you both started acting like everything is okay? How about the way you react to bad news at home vs. in the workplace? The point is that everyone has moments when they suddenly altered their tone and body language due to a third party's presence.

That is how you do it. As soon as you recognize that you have a Murphy in your life, you deliberately put the emotional response aside as if a third party is present. Every time Murphy comes to mind, you set the emotion aside. You know *before* you get a phone call that you *will* get a phone call, and you resolve ahead of time that you cannot be objective about Murphy and that you will set the emotions aside. Make it a game where you are waiting for a Murphy moment to demonstrate that you are in control, objective, and ready to listen. When that call finally comes, the sense of control is automatic. It is a steely-eyed sensation.

Self-awareness is the first ingredient in critical thinking. If you are human, you have strong feelings about a particular set of people, ideas, and values. Critical Thinking cannot exist in those spaces. It may be a cold way to handle situations, but leaders cannot afford to operate off emotions and preconceived sentiments. It will always be evident to outside observers.

Thus far, the focus has been on the "why" aspect of Critical Thinking. Critical Thinking is a bit of a loaded concept and emotion is the most significant barrier to utilizing Critical Thinking as a skill set. From this point forward, the focus will be more on the "how" of Critical Thinking.

2

TRUST BUT VERIFY

INTRODUCTION

The world of superheroes and villains, along with science fiction, has given us a pretty spectacular lineup of supervillains with extraordinary powers and weapons. However, one character out there who, despite not being the mastermind or the leader of the "bad guys," often stands out as the most dangerous and the most frightening. That character is Mystique from the X-Men comic books and movies.

It almost makes my skin crawl to think that someone could perfectly mimic anyone in the world. Whether it would be the highest-ranking person in your organization or a person with whom you share your life and your home, imagine if that person were a determined enemy seeking to destroy you and many others. Imagine putting all your defenses down and openly sharing confidential or highly sensitive information with a trusted friend or authority only to find out later that you were talking to the enemy. Such a person could ultimately access any place on earth and commit any crime they set their mind to.

That is the power of trust, and there are constant security breaches in your mind that flow along lines of trusted sources.

UNFILTERED INFORMATION

The reality is that you spend quite a bit of time with your mind engaged in some form of active defense against "BS." This is because we are lied to constantly by the exaggerated claims of advertising, book covers, movie trailers, TV Promotions, etc. A stick of chewing gum will not suddenly fill your world with rushing psychedelic colors, and most movie trailers and book covers show us the promises of a world that simply do not exist inside the actual emotional content of the story. It is called hype, and we understand it. A thin veneer of cynicism stands between our eyes and pretty much all marketing. Because of that veneer, we are usually applying some degree of critical thinking to the situation.

The problem is trusted sources. For some people, it's an academic degree, a job title, association with a specific university or institution, or perhaps the news anchor that any given person chooses to be their filter into world events. Ultimately, we all establish unspoken trust relationships in the world of information. The more you trust a source of information, the less you will think critically as you listen. More often than not, we settle upon this public figure or that "authority" as someone who is "on our side" and just accept most of what they say. You would be hard-pressed to find a public figure in the world of the information who does not spend a portion of every presentation reminding you why the "other guys" are untrustworthy and have been "debunked."

Strangely, if you turn the channel, you will see the exact opposite sales pitch in action. It is *they* who give you the straight story and *the other guys* who have been "debunked."

As a general rule, you should trust no one when it comes to information since information is a powerful tool in every space of life you enter. Hence wielding information correctly is the secret to success for almost everyone. Motivations are generally self-serving. Then there is a tremendous amount of revenue involved in keeping a loyal audience in the information world. Thus, you are combining money and power in the dispensation of information. Well, what do you think might be happening to your brain if you give unmitigated trust to any single source?

Let's go back to that word, "debunked." Unless you keep your eyes off all national news, you have grown weary of that word, even if you usually agree with the person saying it. However, is there at least one time in the last year when the term was applied to a concept or idea that you just heard about for the first time only one second before? Have you noticed how many words per minute most reporters use when speaking from the studio? Pay attention. They speak fast. One provocative idea is barely uttered before the next is introduced. Within five minutes of these monologues, you should have heard at least three or four things that were worthy of some critical thought, but when did you have the time even to engage your thought processes?

Try this. The next time you hear "debunked," simply turn off the program or turn down the volume and ask yourself some of the following questions:

- Have I seen or heard the conversation or information which debunks the allegedly false idea? Or am I just trusting that it is so?

- Has this idea been around long enough to have its claims honestly looked into, discussed, debated, and pronounced false in an unqualified manner? Or am I merely trusting that *if* there were time to do this, the result would be to falsify the idea.

- Can this idea or topic actually be debunked with publicly available information, or is it more of a "wait and see"? Or am I merely trusting that it is so?

And here is one that works *every time...*

- Aside from opposing opinions, is there extended footage, footage from different angles, or simply other facts that apply to this situation that have not been shared during this segment?

Be careful, though. If you start down this road, you may widen the gap between the news agency of your choice and their advertising revenues.

ACTION AND REACTION

When it comes to news and world events, they all have something in common with the events that you will have to deal with daily as a leader: Action and Reaction.

What do you think of first when you hear that two individuals were in a fistfight?

- Who started it?
- What started it?
- Who was it? (because sometimes it is the person(s) you were suspecting, right?)

The reason these questions come to mind is your intuitive understanding of action and reaction.

But here is the big takeaway. We place moral and ethical worth based on action vs. reaction. Anytime you see or hear about any kind of altercation in your world, or the world at large, *never* accept the first report of "who hit first or why." It will be hard to keep a clear and impartial mind on the facts from that point forward if you do. Keep the attitude of, "okay, *maybe* that's the case."

Think about the difference in terms of moral and ethical worth between these individuals.

- A person trips someone on the bus, but it is a complete accident, and they apologize sincerely. Each person goes their own way politely without further incident.

- A person *attempts* to trip someone on the bus *deliberately* but fails to do so, causing their would-be victim to become angry.

Note: In the first case, a person was affected and fell to the floor with some minor injury, but your sense of moral outrage was minimal, if even present. In the second case, no one was harmed, but you understand why the person was angry.

Now, try this. Look at that second instance and suppose that a while later, you see on a piece of smartphone footage online showing a guy who, "for no reason," just walked over and pushed this other guy on the bus. You might think, "what a psycho," and move on, but if you saw the whole story, it would be a different reaction. What if it was the third day in a row that such an attempt at tripping was made? That is called "baggage" between two people, and it is often left out of the initial reports of altercations.

That is the power of cause and effect. Regardless of where you get your information, you are dealing with an organization that needs views to stay alive. Boring, sensible stories of people acting rationally equal bankruptcy. One way to generate viral content and tidal waves of rage is to show footage that leaves out either the action or the reaction. A violent altercation that makes one party look deranged or motivated by extreme intentions would suddenly look very sensible if the first portion of the conflict were not cut from the presentation.

Don't think a legitimate news organization would do something like that? In decades past, a news organization would take a terrible hit for deliberately reporting anything incorrect. However, the name of the game today is brand loyalty. If you keep the key demographic fired up, they will keep watching even after an otherwise credibility destroying deliberate misrepresentation.

The real point is that you are usually not present when something significant goes down, including events between two or more of your teammates. You will have to rely on what people tell you happened or perhaps incomplete/blurred smartphone footage. Everyone has buddies who know full well the power of getting to you first with their version of the story. It takes a deliberate process to keep first reports, incomplete evidence, or personal baggage separated from the critical thinking process.

Note: If you get it wrong because of some grudge on your part or showing favoritism towards one eyewitness over another, it could be you who ends up on in the boss's office instead of the individual involved in a specific situation.

THE FOLLOWING IS INSPIRED BY ACTUAL EVENTS

This is not a segment about being suspicious of movie banners; this deals with the impact of trust, and how it played out in real life. This is about trust and how trust can be abused.

Your three senior ranking NCOs were hand-selected by the Brigade Commander and Sergeant Major, who both told you that you are in great hands with the "best of the best." Not only that, but your brigade commander's career has a bullet under it, and this leader is likely to be a Four-Star someday, and everyone knows it. You know it. You've seen it and genuinely aspire to be more like them. They are dynamite, and you are thrilled that you have key leaders in your organization with such credibility. As you start the job, you see these NCOs in action, and you see nothing that would take away from the Brigade Commander's assessment. These NCOs are sharp and look the part from their perfectly placed PC caps to their freshly brushed boots. Soldiers respond to them, and they impose the high standards that they seem to embody.

When you speak to Soldiers about the "A-Team" NCOs, the Soldiers light up enthusiastically with a story about how much they appreciate the strong leadership at this unit. However, when speaking with another key leader in the Company about how impressive these NCOs are, the response is lukewarm. For some reason, they don't quite see it the way you do, but hey, to each their own.

(Now, you probably see where this is going based on the setup, but recognize the power of senior positions, recommendations, and appearances in the Army. Trust in a combat-based profession is the default, but under such circumstances, you would be accepting most of what these NCOs tell you about the unit as gospel.)

For a few weeks, you hear about a couple of Soldiers in the unit who have been having some discipline and attitude issues, but it is no big deal; they've been counseled, corrected, and things are looking up. Time goes by, and there is a significant blowout between one of the "troublemakers" and one of the top-notch NCOs. The NCO back briefs you, and the other seniors in the room are nodding their heads. This Soldier is out of control, and UCMJ is probably necessary.

You set all that aside and decide to open your mind and speak to the Soldier one on one. You notice that the NCO in question tries to insert themselves into this one-on-one conversation but backs off as soon as they see you look suspicious. You ask the Soldier if there is something you need to know, and they won't look you in the eye, choosing instead to look at the corner of the room behind you and fume internally.

'Wow,' you think. 'This one is a real special case.'

You gently remind them who is asking the question and request that they look at you and say what they have to say.

They glare at you and then yell, "Just do whatever you want to do. **** it! And **** this company!"

You dismiss the belligerent Soldier and tell them to wait in the orderly room. You've heard enough; this is self-explanatory. However, things did not get like this without a leadership failure of some kind. You already know that you will discipline the Soldier, but you will also do some more digging.

You sit down in your office, and you are about to start typing up the beginning of a counseling statement. You see the Soldier bolt out of the building and sprint across the company area toward the headquarters building. You ask someone to follow them and find out what is going on.

While you anxiously wait, you call in the NCO that had the altercation. They tell you about a remorseful chain of events about all the attitude problems this Soldier exhibits and that the Soldier had a rough childhood, so everyone has been trying to work with them.

You start to sense that the NCO is not entirely straight with you, and then your phone rings.

On the other end of the phone is the Brigade Commander. The unit SHARP rep is in his office, and you are now in the middle of a world-class sexual harassment and sexual assault scandal that, under most circumstances, might make its way to the evening news.

Six months later, all three NCOs are relieved with one-way tickets out of the Army. One of them will spend some time in Leavenworth before parting. There are victims of these NCOs that will likely never recover. Who knows what potential has been lost? Everyone looks terrible, but mostly you look bad because all of this was happening under your nose.

How did you get here? Trust. Impressive people in sacred positions of responsibility took you down the path and played you like a fiddle.

Remember, when people who knew a career criminal are interviewed, they usually say things like, "but they were so friendly/professional/charismatic/charming/etc." Manipulation is an acquired skill, and you may not know who has mastered it until it is too late.

It is easy to look at this story, recognize your own no-nonsense skillset, and believe that it couldn't happen to you, but that is the sort of pride that goeth before a fall. You will build bonds of trust while you serve. Some of those bonds may be forged in fire and blood, but one day, unfortunately, one of those bonds could be betrayed. If you trust someone with your life or if your job implies that you must trust them that much, then it is only reflexive to trust them in other areas.

Trust but verify!

3

LOGICAL FALLACIES: THE ENEMIES OF CRITICAL THINKING

DEFAULTING TO LOGICAL FALLACIES

Logical fallacies are a way of formalizing the war within when it comes to critical thinking. No one is alone when it comes to committing these types of errors. They are so familiar it is easy to generate a universal list of common fallacies that are often easier to see in others than ourselves. Personal stakes in any issue blind us to our logical errors.

There is a need to protect our nearest and dearest held beliefs, AND there is a significant component of our pride associated with making our beliefs and allegiances publicly known. Pride is powerful and admitting we have been wrong about something for a prolonged period, well, it's why wars start and why they sometimes go on for generations. Beliefs are like a poker match in which the stakes increase as you put more chips next to a particular viewpoint or ideology.

Rare is the competitor that can set emotions aside and "know when to fold 'em."

EGOCENTRIC THINKING

Egocentric thinking is a process of forming your thoughts to protect your esteem and reputation. You could say that something is accurate *simply because you believe it.* Try to convince a math teacher that your approach to solving an algorithm *must* be true because of how much you believe it; it probably will not work.

Then we can put our ideological "jerseys" on again and go with the safety in numbers approach. It is *true because WE believe it.* We may take comfort in knowing that "everyone" believes something or that 90% or more of the world's scientists believe_____, but majorities can be wrong, and it is usually the scientist who sees something that no one else did that turns everything upside down: Einstein, Galileo, Pasteur, Darwin, etc. These individuals violated the collective sense of intellectual consensus. History repeatedly shows that one person plus the truth equals a majority, even if it takes a while for everyone else to see it. There is always a price to pay for holding a contrary view, and, in those cases, egocentric thinking has a long leash.

How about, "It is *true because I WANT IT to be true*"? No need to expand on that. There is an inner toddler in almost everyone that sometimes just wants its way. This also tends to happen when in affairs of the heart, family, and friendship. Life is full of discovering things about those closest to us that we just do not want to see and end up ignoring many warning signs.

Then there is a close cousin of the WE factor, and that is the infamous, *"that's the way we've always done it around here."* Unless you are very fortunate, this is the one you have battled personally when assuming a leadership position. Things have been done a certain way for a while, and, for better or worse, everyone is comfortable and knows how to succeed in the current order. Even if your new approach is revolutionary in all the best ways, even if a year from now everyone will be thankful for the changes you made, you can always expect that in the near future, some people will think your ideas are "stupid, non-sensical," or "illogical." Egocentric thinking is also about personal comfort. There should not be a correlation between the experience of being uncomfortable and the experience of encountering a terrible idea, but there is.

Now: "Moving across town makes no sense. All it will do rack up expenses while we transition, and I'm going to miss my friends."

Later: "This new house has made everything better. Our monthly expenses are much less, and I never realized how much I loved gardening until I had space for it."

THE MOST COMMONLY CITED LOGICAL FALLACIES

This book would not be complete without this list, but chances are you have seen them before. Once again, there is just something pervasive about the fact that we often do get things wrong and the reasons why we get them wrong.

Note: These are employed every day by people in every elevated station and authority simply because they work. However, if you engage critical thinking as a deliberate habit, they will stop working on you.

Ad Hominem Attacks

This is just a fancy way of saying, "name calling." Maybe you have noticed how quickly politicians, pundits, and social media icons call their opponents names. What might be thought of as low blows, vicious, outlandish, unfounded, or just way out of bounds are too often the first words of choice? It may seem pointless to just call people names as a means of winning a disagreement, but if the goal is to get an audience on your side, then associating your opponent with a universal evil might be all you need to do. It is sad but true.

The Straw Man

A close cousin of the Ad Hominem is the straw man attack. This one appears far more sophisticated and is therefore far more effective in a surprising number of settings. This is especially true when it mingles with another fallacy that will appear later, i.e., Appeals to Authority. Here is an example.

Councilman Old School is known for his opposition to a new bill that will change several aspects of how local schools run and the costs associated with this approach. He has seen the proposed idea at work in several other school systems and rarely saw the promised results.

Councilman Young Gun gives a speech in front of local media. He states Old School's passionate opposition to the new bill and asserts that Old School does not support public education and wants to see the cities children fall behind other cities. (wow, what a jerk, right?)

The straw man usually substitutes facts with perceptions of intentions. Who cares about facts when you can convince others that someone's heart is in the wrong place? That is why it is called a straw man because a straw man is easy to beat up. An idea might be strong as granite, but by avoiding the substance of an idea in exchange for misconstrued intentions, that granite becomes straw.

Incidentally, the Straw Man gets into "Mind Reading" because you are engaged in hypothesizing another person's intentions, which, in reality, can never be known with any certainty.

The Slippery Slope

In psychological terms, this could be viewed as catastrophic thinking or *Jumping to Conclusions*. This fallacy tends to lead to existentialism or "the world will end unless..."

Here is an example of how the slippery slope might look.

The proposed shopping center will draw thousands of people away from the current shopping areas and locally owned businesses. Within months, national brands will put local business owners into bankruptcy. Before too long, the only people who will be able to afford to shop at the shopping center will be from out of town because everyone around here will be on their way to foreclosure, poverty, and ruin. This proposed shopping center can only do one thing, transforming our community into a demilitarized zone.

False Dilemma or False Dichotomy

Sometimes this is called black and white thinking. That is to say, you are either for us or against us. It may be that Casablanca either is or is not the best movie ever made. However, it would be a false dichotomy to say that those who do not place Casablanca in the top three movies ever made know absolutely nothing about film. How about, "If you do not support candidate X, then you are an evil person"?

Are you starting to see how common these fallacies are? Logical fallacies, for whatever reason, have become the default language of public reasoning. No? Well, here are several more for your consideration.

Circular Reasoning

This is just a way of ending up right where you started but trying to make others believe you took a journey: It is much better to be here because over there is worse, and that other place is the worst of all – Owning a tiger is immoral. I know it is immoral because it is illegal in this state, and because it is unlawful, it is immoral. Suppose you really want to mix it up. In that case, you can replace the obvious boomerang language with intellectual or official-sounding words such as circular reasoning is a fallacy because it is *petitio principii*. Wow, it looks like a lawyer came along and put someone in their place with fancy Latin phrasing. However, *petitio principii* is just Latin for *circular reasoning*.

Speaking of Latin...

Tu Quoque Fallacy

All this means is that a person appeals to some hypocrisy as a means to win an argument. Calling one's opponent a hypocrite is almost a national sport at this point. However, so what if someone is a hypocrite? What does that have to with the validity of their ideas or policy? You may prove that someone does not practice what they preach, but that does not mean that what they preach is incorrect. Most people know that they should exercise more; what is more, they believe it and probably say so when asked. However, if you watch them for a while, you could say that they are hypocrites because they are not exercising more. But what does that have to do with whether or not the benefits of exercise are valid and provable?

How about if a violent criminal gives an interview from prison to talk about how wrong it is to harm others. They are confessed hypocrites, but does that mean they are wrong?

Hypocrisy could indicate that someone is saying something that they know to be false, but without examining the issue on the merits, you could not say for sure.

Hypocrisy more often reveals a lack of character and discipline than it reveals invalid ideas.

Red Herrings

Red Herrings are just sidetracks or unrelated discussion threads. Let's go back to the education debate between the two councilmen.

Councilman Old School: Have you analyzed how much your program will cost or even if it will improve education?

Councilman Young Gun: I refuse to answer that question, coming from a guy whose top donor would likely lose his job on the school board if the education bill passes.

Red herrings are another place where two things can be true and yet be mutually exclusive. It may be true that the top donor has a lot to lose from the new bill being passed into law, but it may also be true that the legislation will not improve the schools. If two things can be accurate simultaneously without any effect on one another, you are dealing with a distraction, not an argument.

Appeal to Authority

As soon as a Constitutional issue arises in the political sphere, you can count the amount of time it takes one network or another to get a Constitutional Scholar from an Ivy League college on air to adamantly and unequivocally support/ oppose in a matter of minutes. Meanwhile, the competing network gets another scholar from the same department at the same university to say the exact opposite. Then the networks will devote time to knowing why their experts are the *real* experts because the other expert is blah, blah, blah. There is so much wrong with appealing to authority.

Authorities, regardless of expertise, have political and ideological axes to grind just like everyone else. They also may have books, speaking engagements, or even their own future political careers to foster. Indeed, most people do not have the mathematical, legal, medical, or scientific expertise to generate their own informed opinions. However, most people can spot someone with a plan or a tendency to avoid direct answers to direct questions.

Appeals to authority work. It may be that a specific brand of socks is no better than a dozen others. Still, for some reason, if the right professional athlete gives a sincere testimonial about those same socks, then most people think, "Well, they can afford the best, so..." Or perhaps, it is the sock company that can afford the best spokesperson.

It is good to know the limits of your own expertise. Still, critical thinking dies when you surrender your right to demand answers to intuitive questions just because someone flashes their academic/professional credentials in your face.

This will be looked at a little more in-depth in an upcoming chapter dealing with a gross miscarriage of justice.

The Bandwagon

If the idea of a Bandwagon sounds old-timey, well, it is. It is loosely connected to the wagon that carried the circus band in the parade and therefore drew people into the circus event. The more people in town that followed the bandwagon to the circus tent, the more the ones who stayed behind feel like they were missing something fun or exciting. Generally, people do not like to miss out on things and certainly do not want to be excluded from the larger community.

Many public campaigns and advertising campaigns attempt to create a perception that there is a certainty to their success, and the sooner you join in, the better. Does anyone remember Google Glass? Or how about a palm-sized computer named The Newton?

While you had better believe that every publicist and marketer since P.T. Barnum knows how to generate bandwagon buzz, it may be best to withstand the strain of jumping on until you have seen some proof positive of validity.

Appeals to Pity

Exploitations of tragedy are too numerous to count. No one likes to see a public figure "standing on the graves" of those who perish in some well-publicized event. Once again, it seems like it is our best qualities that are ripe for exploitation. What could be a better mark of a decent society than those who can be moved to great emotion and compassion for people they have never met? However, when you are in such a state, your defenses may be lower, and your desire to help stop whatever caused the tragedy will be high. This is when legislation containing over a million words starts to go under the banner of a single compassionate sentence. Wait, what are those other 950,000 words in that bill going to do? Well, you would have to be a terrible person to ask such a question, right?

There is another expression that states that sad stories make lousy policy. It is easy to generate support for a development that will help the homeless, but a closer look at the development might reveal just how little good it will do.

Honestly, how many programs, pieces of legislation, or charitable efforts have you seen that promised to fix one thing or another only to see those problems get worse a few years after they pass? What about second and third-order effects. More harm than good is a possibility when pity takes the driver's seat away from critical thinking. It is easy to make another person feel compassion; it is much more difficult to demonstrate why something is true or false.

THE SOKAL AFFAIR AND MORE AFFAIRS.

You may not have heard of the Sokal Affair, but it is a case that proves that all authorities and systems are prone to human failings and creative ways that insiders expose their peers.

When it comes to hot button issues and intellectual authority, few things rise above the fray as much as words like "academic journals" and "peer reviewed studies." We expect that the checks, balances, rigors, competition, and underlying ethics of scientific research would almost assure that peer-reviewed publications are the closest thing to granite that we could build an argument or understanding upon.

However, researchers are human and are prone to both desires for success, wealth, influence, fame, and fears of exclusion, mockery, loss of reputation, etc. The process of peer review and editorial oversight should intervene, but all systems are prone to failure.

Enter Alan Sokal, a physics professor at New York University, who believed that political agendas were allowing garbage science to enter society as reliable data. To prove his point, he crafted an article that was complete nonsense but used a lot of politically desirable language. His conclusions were hyperbolic and should have thrown red flags into the editors' minds. Sokal did this as an experiment to see if the article would get published.

Perhaps it was unethical to put forth a false paper deliberately, or maybe you could call this entrapment. Still, if peer-review and academic rigor are as good as everyone thinks they are, then the article should fail.

It did not.

Once the article was published, Alan Sokal came forward with the truth and reason for doing what he did. As a result, there was quite a bit of soul searching, and editorial review processes were tightened up. You might call what he did performance or protest art which resulted in institutional change. Another result of this was a new hobby for academic pranksters in the form of would-be Sokals who prod the system for weaknesses regularly.

Three such disciples gained recent fame by writing 20 phony research papers loaded with all the things that the editors wanted to hear. Over the course of one year, these papers went out to various respected peer-reviewed publications. The results: Seven were published. That is not bad, but there is a lot of room for junk science in the best journals.

Once again, the point is that leaders should not trust any authority blindly. The tendency to bow out as soon as Ph.D. or academic publication flashes on the screen is a terrible practice.

For more on this, go to a website called retractionwatch.com. There are stunning numbers of published science articles that end up being retracted for invalid findings and outright criminal fraud each year. One big takeaway is that if scientific publications' rigors can fall into turning a blind eye to bad ideas, then so can anyone. To err is human, but there is something divine about looking at your thoughts and beliefs critically.

The entire situation exposed by Sokal and others is comparable to the emergence of toxic leadership climate and "tell the boss what they want to hear" that puts lives or livelihood at risk.

Keep your door open. Somewhere in your organization is a Sokal who can help you see your leadership philosophy and agenda in a whole new light.

4

MUTUAL EXCLUSIVITY

INTRODUCTION

This book covers the concept of common logical fallacies which are generally in wide distribution. Much like the list of things which are good for tomato plants to thrive, there is nothing very original to add. They are what they are and pretty much always have been. The only problem with such lists, unless you are dedicating yourself to them full-time as part of a professional life, is that they are hard to remember. By the time we graduate high school, it seems we should know what year Abraham Lincoln was born and also what year the Civil War ended, but memorizing is a dead-end when it comes to long term retention.

What usually helps is boiling everything down to one over-arching principle. You might use a phrase or an acronym to remember the principle or process.

Another way to approach a complex set of ideas is to find one practical tool, or perhaps a litmus test. For example: Is it an "opportunity" if the gist of their offer is for *me* to pay *them* up front and then work hard in hopes I will get it back?

WHAT IS MUTUAL EXCLUSIVITY?

Simply put: Just because *this* does not necessarily mean *that*. i.e., false connections between two different things.

"John, you must be high if you think you have time learn to play the piano in six months." To which John can reply, "The fact that I am high has nothing to do with how much time I'm going to commit to the piano in the next six months."

Or perhaps:

"Are you here to play chess or crack your knuckles?" he demanded. "I'm here to play chess *and* crack my knuckles," John replied smugly.

Aside from some humorous anecdotes, a mutually exclusive statement would look more like: It is possible for the professor to be both an authority on lung cancer *and* be completely wrong about the recommended treatment. Such a statement gets at the heart of the fallacy of appealing to authority outright. The opposite problem of discounting someone due to lack of expertise can also be addressed this way: It is possible that a junior team leader knows nothing about operational planning *and* can still tell us exactly where we might go wrong on the first phase of the plan.

When it comes to critical thinking or avoiding logical fallacies and thinking traps, the most efficient habit is to phrase the issue as a mutually exclusive statement. If you are paying attention, you will be amazed by what you see in both news media and social media when it comes to mutually exclusive ideas…or the outright rejection of them. Isn't it pretty standard stuff to hear something like, "Senator X, do you really expect us to believe that in your *one year* as a United States Senator that you have discovered how to fix _____?"

Or perhaps, "Of course, a millionaire like you, Congressman X, (insert subtle tone of righteous indignation) wouldn't really know, would you?"

Information related to current events is often geared at provoking emotions, lumping persons or ideas into negative associations, or allowing us to believe we can know what some public figure was *thinking* or *what was in their heart* when they did something. This of course is almost always the same two equations:

They are on my team = They were thinking of creating world peace and ending hunger because love and goodness are always in their heart.

They are not on my team = They dance with the devil in the pale moonlight and want puppies to die of cancer.

All of that is a bit ridiculous, but is it really? Just take a moment of introspection and consider the last guy who was president that you really opposed. Now finish this sentence, "However, I was very supportive of the following three things he did..." Now how about this? "I hated it when he _____ because he knew that it would _____" Unless you are a rare kind of 21st century American, then at least one of those phrases hung you up. Note, the trap on the second one was not identifying an action you hated, but having a great deal of certainty regarding what the former or current president was *thinking*.

Honestly, most people know their spouse, their sibling, or their best friends pretty well and even then, they could probably not tell you what those people were *thinking* during any given action. If you have overwhelming certainty about how a person you've never met thinks through decisions and what motivates them, then you have probably been sold something...and it might have been in the same aisle as propaganda.

How often have you looked back on your own actions years later to discover that even you, at that time, did not actually understand what was motivating you? Maybe you were convinced that you were up to something noble, but in retrospection you realized you were really trying to gain security, esteem, or favor. Life is complicated, everyone is human, and humans never have all the information they need prior to making a decision. If you remember that, it can help you restrain the urge to emotionally commit anger or frustration to a stranger who happens to be famous. Which also makes it easier to apply mutual exclusivity.

Let's revisit those two hypothetical political statements from a couple paragraphs back.

"Senator X, do you really expect us to believe that in your *one year* as a United States Senator that you have discovered how to fix _____?"

It is possible that Senator X is both a new Senator *and* has been able to see a solution that everyone else missed.

"Of course, a millionaire like you, Congressman X, (insert subtle tone of righteous indignation) wouldn't really know, would you?"

It is possible that Senator X is both a millionaire *and* does, in fact, know.

In the case of Senator X, it is likely that his plan is naïve, short-sited, or simplistic. You wont know until you've heard him out and given him a fair shot at addressing the problem. Shutting something down or setting your mind and emotions against something or someone before you've heard them out all but guarantees that you will reject it no matter what. If you are rejecting something because of an undefined concept of how long someone has been on the job versus the merits of the idea itself, then critical thinking was not part of your equation.

Now the second notion:

It is true that someone can only really understand how something feels if they experience it for themselves. Therefore, the idea that Senator X is a millionaire (and for the sake of argument always has been) and therefore does not "know," has validity. So long as the point of contention revolves around emotions, empathy, or psychological needs, then it is probably best to let those who have *been there* do the talking. However, a statement like "because you wouldn't really know, would you?" can also be a convenient way to shut someone down that you just don't want to hear or be heard.

Maybe Senator X is trying to stop abusive lending practices and his critic (secretly) owns stock in the short-term loan agency being discussed. Stranger things have happened. If it were so, then you would see the argument much differently than if you take the emotional bait of marginalizing one participant based on socioeconomic status.

A broken clock is right twice a day. Give people a chance. People we do not like can be spot on. Being correct has no scientific correlation to likeability. Sir Isaac Newton was notoriously unpleasant to be around.

MUTUAL EXCLUSIVITY MEETS LOGICAL FALLACIES

Now, it is time to do a quick paring of the mutually exclusive statement with each of the logical fallacies presented earlier. This should demonstrate how getting used to using this one phrasing device can radically enhance your critical thinking abilities.

Egocentric Thinking: Something is true because *we believe* it is true or because we *need* it to be true. The mutually exclusive statement solution for this is probably the best one since keeping this statement at the front of your thoughts could change everything.

Solution: It is possible for (insert opposing viewpoint logic) to be devastating to my beliefs and for that same logic to be true.

Ad Hominem Attacks: "Name Calling"

Solution: It is possible for someone to both be a stupid, immoral jerk *and* be correct or truthful about any given issue.

Straw Man: The tactic of connecting an individual's opinion to a moral fault by way of a giant leap of logic. Example: Councilman Old School does not support the new education bill because he "wants kids to get left behind." Note the additional element of mind reading. Does anyone know what someone else "wants" when forming an opinion?

Solution: It is possible for Councilman Old School to be both opposed to a new education program *and* highly motivated by creating the best education system possible.

Slippery Slope: Akin to jumping to conclusions. "If we go to the beach, we'll get too much sun, we'll get sunburned, we'll suffer for days from burnt skin, get skin cancer, and we'll die."

Solution: It is possible to both enjoy a trip to the beach *and* minimize sun exposure. Additionally, it is possible to get a sunburn *and* live a long healthy life for decades without getting cancer.

False Dilemma or False Dichotomy: "You're either for us or against us." "If you don't like Casablanca, then you don't know anything about movies." "If you disagree with me about politics, then you are an evil person."

Solution: It is possible to both sharply disagree with someone *and* nonetheless have similar values seeking positive goals.

Circular Reasoning: Owning a tiger is immoral because it is illegal and illegal means immoral.

Solution: It is possible that something may be both illegal *and* moral, or both legal *and* immoral.

Tu Quoque Fallacy: The idea that because someone is a hypocrite, then their beliefs or philosophy is proven false.

Solution: It is possible to both fail at eating a healthy diet *and* to be correct about the benefits of healthy eating.

Red Herring: Unrelated arguments, rabbit trails, distractions, and side-tracks. "I refuse to answer your objection, because it turns out your top donor will lose his job on the school board if the education bill passes."

Solution: It is possible for the objection to both be valid *and* that the new program will cost a friend their job.

Appeal to Authority, the Bandwagon, and Pity: These are the notions of high social status, or a majority, or feeling empathy toward someone equals valid ideas.

Solution 1: It is possible for multiple Ivy League professors to agree about an idea *and* for that idea to be false or inaccurate.

Solution 2: It is possible for "everyone" to agree about something *and* for "everyone" to be completely wrong.

Solution 3: It is possible to have genuine empathy for a crime victim *and* believe that the viral political solution will create more victims.

5

NORMALCY BIAS

OUT OF THE BOX AND CHALLENGING THE NORM

Critical Thinking is basically loophole thinking. It wants to find that little space to break an idea apart. It is a way of thinking that is unfettered by rules, convention, prejudice, or pride. It asks both "why?" and "why not?" Critical Thinking does not care if it has no friends or fails to fit in. Critical thinking has no friends except the ruthless cold pursuit of truth. It will choose to entertain horrible possibilities and ugly ideas simply to get to the bottom of them and defeat them or accept them as ultimate reality. Critical Thinking is willing to argue any side of any argument for the sake of understanding them better.

NORMALCY BIAS

Maybe right now you are in the comfort of your home with a smart phone nearby, climate control, hot and cold running water, and contemplating any number of dining options involving foods from any part of the world that are within a reasonable distance and budget. There are kings and emperors of old who lacked most of these things. However, we take them for granted and frequently complain about any number of modern inconveniences. That is because our 21st standard of living is "normal." Much of what we see and do would mesmerize those who lived in the past as we might be mesmerized by those things which might one day be normal despite being unimaginable now.

Somewhere at some time there was the first commercial flight with WiFi provided to passengers by the Airline. Now it is hard to imagine a time when you could not access the internet while on a plane. There was a time when one Bluetooth device connected to another Bluetooth device for the first time in what would be a miniature techno revolution. Now, a world without Bluetooth might bring about comments referencing the "stone age."

Normalcy Bias is natural and basically unavoidable. However, it is also a component of Ethnocentric thinking or the idea that your culture is superior to others because_. What could be better proof that current culture is superior to cultures in the past because we have access to so many amazing comforts and gadgets?

Normalcy Bias is the root of accepting or rejecting ideas for the simple reason that they feel normal or right according to what we are used to. Abnormal ideas, conduct, clothing styles, etc. easily come across as strange, crazy, immoral, uncomfortable, inferior, out of touch, out of date, etc. If you somehow jumped into a society 100 years ago, 100 years from today, or even 100 miles away, you would almost certainly come across as abnormal.

Remember the reference to "because that's the way we do things around here"? Such a statement is another expression of Normalcy bias. A bad idea = change because change alters what is normal. Of course, a new idea could objectively be bad, but simply becoming indignant or insulted because a deviation from normalcy is introduced is one way to make decisions, but it is also the enemy of critical thinking.

Moral compasses are all too often connected to perceived normalcy. It is "the current year," and hence it is hard to believe that someone still believes_(insert "old" moral construct here)_____." It could be true that a certain moral view is both relatively new in human history and long overdue, or it could be that it is only normal in our current space in time.

There is an idea that we can judge times past because we see things a certain way now, why can't those in the past jump forward and judge us for seeing things different from what they considered normal? Barring a moral authority greater than any given culture, society, or time, everything else is just a connection to normalcy.

Here is what that means. Depending on when and where you live, any one of the following things is Normal: Being a Christian, being a Muslim, being an Atheist, being well-fed, not knowing where the next meal will come from, eating meat, being a vegan, driving a car, never driving a car, etc., etc.

By contrast, for each of those times and places, anyone who shows up with sharply different views or expectations will be abnormal and met with some hostility and indignation.

Perhaps you have heard something like, "Well, yeah, John Adams had strong Christian beliefs, but that is only because that's what people believed then." Which could prompt, "So our tendency to keep our religious beliefs out of our public life is basically what people believe *now*. We're all in the same boat."

The point is not to say that truth does not exist or that current baseline beliefs are wrong just because they are new. The point is to take time and examine the degree to which you believe what you believe simply because of normalcy and the cultural pressure and biases that imposes.

Think about it this way. If a major crime happened in your neighborhood or near your workspace and the police asked you if you saw anything suspicious in the last 72 hours, well, isn't that just another way of asking you if you have seen anything that was *not normal*?

THE OVERTON WINDOW

Normalcy Bias is connected to the Overton Window. The Overton Window is basically the spectrum of ideas that people in a given time or place are willing to accept. The Overton Window can encompass volatile issues such as sexuality, economic systems, gender issues, etc. But it can also be something as simple as whether or not men should wear hats as a standard part of wearing a suit, should gel their hair, or wear skinny ties. Fashion is very much in the Overton Window and not surprisingly, many fashion trends are linked to major shifts in political views and religious sentiments.

We would probably like to think that any given politicians' success would have to do with the degree to which they embrace a strong sense of vision, but all too often it boils down to how well they perceive the Overton Window. This leads to a trickle down of logical fallacies in which pursuing the things that are easy to digest, support, and talk about in language that is highly acceptable takes the place of determining what is so in language that needs to be stated.

Subsequently, far too many things are called "brave," when they in fact require no courage at all to say. A statement that cannon blasts dead center through the Overton Window may be highly applauded and widely distributed, but is also a very safe shot.

6

THE SHERLOCK HOLMES MIND

INTRODUCTION

Sherlock Holmes endures, much like Einstein, as an icon of deductive power and the power of human reason to solve seemingly impossible riddles. There is already plenty written about why he is seen as the epitome of reason. Often, the focus is on Sherlock's infamous "mind palace," because of his ability to mentally store vast amounts of knowledge for quick reference and cross reference. However, this becomes less and less interesting in a world where everyone holds an infinite data search device in the palm of their hands. It is really not so much about what information you have, but what you do with the information.

Sherlock Holmes, much like Einstein, was surrounded by other research/investigative professionals with access to the same facts as he, but with remarkably different results. The two keys to Sherlock's success are a nearly inhuman capacity for observation (for example: noting a specific type of small stain on the jacket of a passerby) and eliminating bias from his reasoning. The second key is the focus of this book and is often associated with Critical Thinking.

Before going into any detail, reference to Sherlock Holmes is perfect place to touch on something extremely important to the modern mind. Sherlock Holmes is a fictional character whose achievements exist in an alternate reality. The same could be said of his literary peers such as Edgar Allan Poe's Detective who predates Holmes, Auguste Dupin, as well as Agathe Christie's Hercule Poirot and Miss Marple. Fiction is a world where the author controls the physics, chance, weather, and socio-political realities of the world. Therefore, the characters are often privy to the right piece of information at the right time or simply likewise find themselves in a certain part of the landscape at the right time, etc.

There has probably never been a time in history where the average person has access to, or partakes of so much story telling in the form of streaming movies and television shows. Ask yourself how often a political, religious, or other ideological element is brought into the stories you consume. If you consider indirect references, then the answer starts to align with Orwell's assessment that:

All Art is Propaganda.

At first glance, this seems extreme and ridiculous, but when you consider the implications of why characters, settings, and the rules of a fictional world are in place, you realize that the author is always saying something without really saying it. This could be summed up as context and pretext. But no matter how you slice it, it is all *convenient*. Even simple, brainless action sequences present us with ideas that those who are in the right will prevail and have fate on their side.

All of this is to say two things. One, be very cautious to derive strong beliefs about your world based on the machinations of a fictional world and completely made-up "good" and "evil" character types. Two, Sherlock Holmes gives us wonderful insights into the power of reason, but we also need to appreciate the conveniences of his situations.

 In the case of the Red-Headed League, Sherlock Holmes was asked to help a red headed man, Mr. Wilson, figure out what happened to an organization that up until recently was providing him with gainful employment, but suddenly vanished without a trace. It was an organization which supposedly wanted to provide opportunities and assistance to red headed people in a predominantly blond and brunette world.

Mr. Wilson described how he responded to an ad in a paper and fought his way through at least a hundred applicants who were crowding around the hiring office. After an interview, the man was selected due to the particularly brilliant hue of his red hair. From that day forward, he was to report to the same building where he interviewed and copy texts. It was brainless work, but the money was excellent. The only thing that made working for the league unpleasant was the degree to which they demanded that he stay at the site for the entire duration of the shift and was not even allowed to leave the building. The whole thing might have seemed like a scam except Mr. Wilson did not have to part with any money or belongings at any time. Who would pull such a prank at such great cost?

What's your bias in this situation? Mr. Wilson shouldn't worry too much about it and it doesn't sound like any real crime was committed anyway? Take the money and run? It couldn't be a real hoax because it is too improbable and too expensive? Red-headed people aren't picked on badly enough to justify such an organization?

There is nothing wrong with any of these points of view and they are all valid, but spending too much time on any one of them is time that the sleuth does not have. The story has a built-in ticking clock and Sherlock's ability to dispassionately and quickly sort through which considerations are important and which are not.

There is real bias in being too dismissive of people's concerns or observations because you think they sound ridiculous, or because they made more money than you last month, or perhaps they just sound like a cry-baby. The Red-Headed league is good case study because Holmes does something that most of us do not; he sets aside the calloused indifference and cynicism of living in a busy world. The point here is that biases that make headlines are easy to contemplate, but subtle ones such as cynicism often go completely unchecked.

In this case, instead of focusing on the name of the person who did the hiring, the history of an actual Red-Headed league, the unimportance of the Mr. Wilson's situation, or even the possibility that the man was, once again, being singled out for practical joke because of having red hair, Sherlock focused on where the man might be if he weren't at work copying texts.

A little bit of critical thinking seemed warranted when an otherwise generous and easy-going arrangement has one such strict requirement. Why such a focus on never leaving the building? Sounds more like a form of voluntary confinement. What could be the purpose other than to keep the unwitting participant away from someplace else?

Of course, looking at the situation that also meant that it would also be true that the man was specifically targeted for this outcome. That would mean that the ad was a hoax, the crowd of people applying for the job would have had to have been at least partially in on it, and Mr. Wilson's awareness of the ad, as well as his responding to the ad, could not be left to chance.

This led Holmes to focus on Mr. Wilson's usual location (a small pawn shop which he owed), how he heard about the ad (a new employee who showed it to him and greatly encouraged him to respond), and what part of town Mr. Wilson's shop was located (right next to a bank).

From there it did not take long that to realize that the small fortune spent on the hoax was nothing compared to what could be stolen from digging a tunnel into a bank and then sneaking in at night. This also meant that the new employee was probably the mastermind of the whole thing and that the plan may have been in place long before ever showing up to work at the pawn shop.

From there, Sherlock wanted to make sure he caught the entire crew in the act of robbing the bank and knew that time was short due to the sudden disappearance of the Red Headed League. Then, in what could have been a chaotic scene in which everything went wrong, Holmes and a couple of law enforcement officers waited in the bank's basement for the criminals to show up. One short action scene later, the good guys won without any serious injury to the characters we care about the most.

And wasn't it a good thing that this elaborate plan did not include just one more day's pay and work for Mr. Wilson? If it did, then they would have gotten away with it. How convenient. Of course, this matter of convenience gives us the perfect point in time to put Holmes in a situation where he must unravel a complex situation quickly in a way that no one else could.

Now, compare this to a real-life case in which a horrifying tragedy that has been widely viewed as a gross mishandling of investigative duties. A case were cynical police insisted on pushing evidence in a statistically likely scenario in order to quickly close a case. Here are the primary facts which investigators had during the first 24 hours.

In 2004, a three-year-old girl named Riley Fox went missing from her home in Wilmington, Illinois. Her father and brother were in the house but allegedly asleep at the time she went missing. The front and back doors were slightly ajar, but no signs of forced entry or struggle. Shortly thereafter, a search effort discovered Riley Fox's body along the banks of a nearby river. Of note, the Fox family's house was across the street from another house which had been recently burglarized.

Now, imagine as a police officer working in this jurisdiction you respond to a suspected suicide attempt. Upon entering the scene, you discover a young man who is suffering the side effects of a deliberate pain killer overdose. He is violently ill and barely intelligible but manages to ask you if you have found out anything more about that missing girl.

What would you do with that inquiry? What steps might you take after handling the health emergency on the scene?

Later on, police discover that the rear door of the Fox's house was in disrepair and could not be fully secured. They also discovered that a red car had been seen in the neighborhood frequently despite no one knowing whose it was. But they also discovered blurry grey security camera footage taken around 2 a.m. that could resemble the father's pick-up. Then there was more evidence found near the body in the form of a pair of men's shoes that had been marked with what is likely their owner's name on the inside. You can almost make out that the letters are E-B-Y. The father's name is Kevin Fox. They are not his size.

Since the house had no signs of struggle, no other missing items, or even indications of a thief searching through drawers etc. to find valuables, and since family members are often the guilty parties in such cases, Kevin Fox became the prime suspect. The shoes, the mysterious red car, and the fact that the father had not said or done anything out of the ordinary to that point were set aside. Keven Fox was brought in for 14 hours of intensive questioning which ended with complying to a statement generated by the investigators as "the most likely chain of events." It was a written confession.

It may seem crazy to sign a confession to a violent crime you did not commit, but many people do it every year in the midst of the psychological effects of prolonged questioning. It was a confession none the less.

Kevin Fox was found guilty and sentenced to prison for the crime of assaulting and killing his own daughter. He would be in prison for several years.

What do you think?

Remember that suicide attempt. The person who overdosed on pain killers was named Scott Eby, he drove a red car, lived a few minutes from the Fox family, had a history of house burglary and many other crimes for which he served time in prison, and he *was* trying to commit suicide out of the guilt for what he did to Riley Fox. It seemed that Eby did everything he possibly could to lead the investigation to himself. Even then, if Eby had not called his mother from prison on a recorded line to vent his concerns that the police may figure out what he had done, we may still not know it was him.

You have heard of dumb criminals who make investigators' job way too easy. Scott Eby falls just short of being a classic dumb criminal, but the obviousness of his involvement was almost at that level. The Fox family will spend the rest of their lives wondering why investigators did not do any of the following:

- Research the criminal backgrounds of everyone within 2 to 5 miles of the crime the victim's home and crime scene.

- Follow up on the reports of the red car and also research red cars registered in the local area

- Complete a background check on Scott Eby at the time of his suicide attempt

- Run a search on last names that resembled the letters on the inside shoe

- Inquire as to why a person in the midst of an overdose would be asking about a missing child

  Etc, etc, etc.

This all goes to demonstrate the power of bias and being set in your own idea of how and why things happened. Or in short, you can't find something unless you are looking, so despite the very large breadcrumbs and "alarms" that the real killer left behind, the case (at least in the minds of some investigators) was already closed.

Fewer things could be farther from the Sherlock Holmes mindset and modern social media culture. Gossip, headlines, and subsequent volatile emotional responses move faster than light across the entire culture. Before anyone can even wonder if what they are seeing is based in reality, there are already highly paid media figures setting up expert panels to stoke the flames before a national audience. It doesn't matter whether or not a scandalous photo was taken years earlier and in an entirely different context. By the time anyone even wonders about the photos validity there will fully vested emotions and entrenched life or death levels of commitment to party-line positions.

One great way to move closer to the Sherlock Holmes mindset and therefore Critical Thinking as a way of life is to resist the temptations to take every bit of "rage-bait" that the internet and television drop in front of you. Commit yourself to holding all emotional responses back until you know more. Set the story or issue aside for 24 hours and then see the latest updates. You will find more often than not that what people reacted to at first has almost nothing to do with what actually happened. However, the changes in facts will NOT usually change the entrenched, fully committed views of most media participants and millions of followers. This is because once you commit a strong emotional response to a situation, it is very difficult to make it back.

Ever been in fight with a loved one and then realized in the middle that you were actually wrong, only to find yourself *not* de-escalating and instead avoiding having to acknowledge you were wrong? Maybe even years later you are still not able to fully admit you had it wrong? Emotions can superglue you to a viewpoint. It is easy to keep an open mind and adapt to new facts if you keep them in check.

Consider the following:

When the Costa Concordia sank sideways into shallow water near Greece, it was a media sensation. News and internet agencies were fighting for viewers and were trying to keep them engaged for as long as possible. As a result, much of the footage and captured video portraying tables and chairs crashing back and forth across a ballroom floor, water gushing down stairwells, etc. were pulled in from previous events on other cruise ships in recent years. Those older film clips were posted to the Costa Concordia event without any disclaimers. People watching those captured videos were having an emotional response to them and staying engaged. It shaped the way the felt about the event and shaped their opinions about those involved. But it was all for show. Nothing more than a way to keep people emotionally invested in their screen time over that tragic event. Of course, the actual event was probably much worse than the contrived footage, but the point is to be careful of all initial reports and commentary when so many people are vying for the same audience and ad revenue.

Wildfires are a political flashpoint due to environmental concerns across the globe. However, this means that the shoot first, ask questions later way in which politics can ruin everything gets involved. You may remember in 2019 there was quite a bit of news coverage about wildfires in the Amazons. Celebrities tweeted, world leaders demanded action, several governments declared emergencies, and millions of dollars in aid started to flow. One interesting fact is that at that exact time there were five times more fires burning across central Africa than in the Amazon. At the very least, the flurry of social media may have been burying a larger tragedy from public view.

However, once journalists hit the ground and began to research the activity in the Amazon firsthand, they discovered that most of the fires were due to agricultural activity in rural areas and not in the rainforest. The fires were part of a deliberate effort to clear brush and nourish the soil. A common practice since the dawn of farming. It is considered a safe practice since humidity levels in the Amazon generally prevent unwanted spread of the agricultural fires. The most common photos shared by celebrities and other top social media influencers were from other actual emergency events from previous years (20 to 30 years earlier, and in some cases, not even from the Amazon).

There was quite a bit of emphasis on the Amazon due to the thought that, due to the immense amount of vegetation, it produces as much as 20% of our breathable air and thereby can be viewed as the "lungs of the earth." However, Dan Nepstad, the head of the United Nation's IPCC (Intergovernmental Panel on Climate Change) did not agree. Once the "lungs of the earth" idea became prominent he pointed out that the Amazon is also responsible for a great deal of oxygen utilization which results in few net gains for the world as a whole.

More social media chimed in with one celebrity account citing that the Amazon fires represented an almost unprecedented disaster the likes of which had not occurred for at least 20,000 years. However, data from the previous 20 years placed 2019 into a perfectly average bandwidth when it comes to wildfires.

There is more, but the point is made. Of course, this sort of presentation generates strong emotions of one kind or another in most audiences. Therefore, this is a place where the principle of mutual exclusivity needs to be inserted.

- It is possible to both accept that the 2019 Amazon wildfires were misrepresented in western media and still believe or know that there are serious climate issues.

- It is possible to both recognize the need to get the word out when something indicative of climate change is happening and still be critical of overblown or unsubstantiated events.

- It is possible too that the Amazon wildfires story has no connection to climate change and that climate change is real.

However, it is always good to wait a little bit before fully vesting your emotions into the next viral social issue on social media. If you really care about an issue, then you want the most credibility over the long term. Failing to call out those who create more doubt or embarrassment just because they are on your "team" is counterproductive in the end.

In 2012, there was a campaign to raise awareness of an Ugandan warlord named Joseph Kony. There does not seem to be any debate about the evils of Joseph Kony's atrocities over the years. If you have seen *Tears of the Sun* starring Bruce Willis, then you have some idea. The campaign was produced by Invisible Children led by Jason Russell. To make a long story short, Jason Russell had obvious good intentions but much of the effort was corny and somewhat cringeworthy to watch. The campaign was an overnight success and the team behind it were not ready for the sudden fame and attention.

As is the case in many situations, there was a natural backlash and wave of criticism of the 2012 campaign. It was the sort of social media phenomenon where the everyone wanted to get on the critical band-wagon. In the midst of this, an influencer with millions of followers posted a video in which she described how her mom laughed about Joseph Kony because he, "died five years ago."

Now, it is hard to imagine something simpler to fact check than whether or not an infamous public figure is alive or dead, but if you have more than a million followers, you must be right. Kony was most definitely still alive but despite this, millions of people now believed he was dead thanks almost exclusively to that social media post. When there is "blood in the water" and a feeding frenzy begins, Critical Thinking evaporates. Of course, it is possible that both Kony was still alive in 2012 *and* that Invisible Children was worthy of criticism.

However, it is yet another way in which consuming information in the 21st century turns our best instincts and strongest emotions into our worst enemies.

The difference between a person whose life is relentlessly destroyed by social media and a person who learns from a simple mistake can be measured to the degree to which they are held accountable for what they actually did and also what they actually got right. The tendency to see someone as 100% evil since birth because they simply misquoted something or misread a situation is a sad part of our reality. As a critical thinker, you can be part of the solution.

Perhaps you know of many more similar examples in both mainstream and independent media. Perhaps you or someone you care about have personally been hurt by being misrepresented in the public square. The good news is that these moments in human history seem to come and go. Perhaps the next backlash to go viral will be an anti-hysteria movement.

Always keep in mind that those who control a media channel (regardless of size or influence) have something in common with novelists and screen writers: the ability to construct the physics and happenstance of the world they portray.

FINAL THOUGHTS

Sherlock Holmes, at least in one portrayal, described himself as a "high functioning sociopath." This was intended to demonstrate both the fact that his intellectual gifts are powered by an absence of emotional connection, and also that he is as ruthless and honest when looking at himself as he is with the world around him. There is a brutal honesty without regard for losing friends in such a statement. This might intersect with a bit of a Simon Cowell mindset.

As you go throughout your day and are exposed to a thousand different human interactions and ten thousand bits of media related information, go ahead and start taking an honest assessment of your own beliefs. As soon as your emotions jump to a new place because of something around you, just ask yourself why. As soon as you realize that you are having a hard time with another person, consider that it may be more than just the facts at hand. Only you can do this. But here are some things to consider.

- Am I for or against this just because I need my party or team to be in the right?

- Am I for or against this just because of the race, gender, or sexuality of the people involved?

- Am I for or against this just because of how I see the socioeconomics as presented?

- Is my view of what is moral or immoral limited to who agrees with me and who does not?

- Do I tolerate terrible behavior from public figures just because calling them out would make "the other team" look good?

- Do I think that someone is honest or credible just because I like them or sympathize with them?

- Is someone trying to gain my sympathy or make me like them just so I will overlook and even accept their terrible behavior?

- Is someone an expert because of their experience, profession, education, and proven track record, or do I simply accept that a PhD plus agreeing with me is the way to determine credibility?

And let's all hope that one does not need to be a sociopath in order to be a cool, clearheaded critical thinker.

7

CHALLENGING DEEPLY HELD BELIEFS OR BELIEVING VS. ACTUALLY BELIEVING

TEAM JERSEYS VS. CRITICAL THOUGHT

Religion and politics ruin everything. People can be getting along wonderfully, and then somehow either religion or politics gets in the mix and then there are problems. People find it hard to agree to disagree when opposition to your deepest held beliefs feels like a threat to civilization itself. (NOTE: if a threat to your beliefs feels like a threat to civilization itself, it may be a sign that stepping back a little bit and broadening your lens could be good for your well-being).

This section is not a critique of any political or religious beliefs (or the concept of those beliefs), but a moment to reflect on the power that those fundamental beliefs have on how we see the world. It is not so much that some people are "glass half empty" and others are "glass half full" but really, whether the person holding the glass is wearing our team's jersey.

There is a mayoral candidate in Illinois who simply refuses to adopt a political party, endorse, or campaign with known party candidates, or even speak to national wedge issues that do not concern her city. It is clear from watching public events, interviews, and traffic on her social media that most people do not know how to feel about her or anything she is trying to do. There is a distinct impression that people do not know *how* to think about a politician or a policy unless there is a party affiliation to go with it.

- Is it better to cut a tax or increase it?

- Should we commit troops to a new conflict or seek out other means of influence?

- Should one sector of the economy be valued and protected over another?

- How much wealth equals "rich," and how should they be taxed?

- Does one type of government assistance actual hurt the people it is supposed to help?

In a vacuum, a person should be able to look at each of these questions (and a thousand more) and arrive at a unique blend of complex answers. However, parties and close communal allegiances tend to do that for us. We put on our team jersey and find ourselves in ideological lock step with our team. Suddenly, millions of people can look at that complex list and tick the box 90% or more identical to each other while becoming highly intolerant of opposing views or information.

Isn't it strange to see so many people agree so passionately about a wide array of complex and diverse issues? Isn't it even stranger that within two to four years, the exact ideas all those people violently opposed a few years ago, they now passionately support? And all these millions of people made this ideologically polar switch at the same time and in complete agreement with one another. It is very hard to see how the tide is moving you and your fellow swimmers until you look back and note that the beach is gone. Well, you're all in the same place, so you can't all be wrong, right? Start asking those hard questions. It is the only way to know.

Religious affiliation (or an adamant anti-religious sentiment) often has the same effect. The same power of affiliation can be applied to close co-workers, families, neighborhoods, etc. Call it human nature but running with the pack or the herd comes way more naturally than Critical Thinking. Even a cursory glance at the cruel laws of nature will show you that it is both difficult and dangerous to be a lone wolf. Sometimes we know we are wrong, but those who are right are out in the cold and exposed to threats. There is a difference between recognizing that a fact is a fact and being willing to suffer for that fact.

Such a moral tug of war is deeply entwined in the worst moments of history. Mobs will flood into a moral panic or a "witch hunt," knowing that the persecution is wrong, but also that speaking against the persecution leads to persecution. However, one MAJOR fallacy regarding witch hunts is to get hung up on the religious aspect of the original witch hunts in Salem. This fallacy leads to movements that perpetrate witch hunts but cannot see the comparison because they are opposed to "organized religion" or Christianity, or religion in general. The key to a witch hunt is not the motivation, but the methodology. For reference, examine Saddam Hussein's rise to power or the daily conduct of Stalin's regime. There are countless movements with large body counts whose witch hunt methods were highly effective despite an avowed anti-religious sentiment. French Revolution anyone?

The point is to remember that you are not immune to evil doing because you are "on the right side of history." Every tyrannical, blood thirsty regime you could flee from was filled to the brim with loyal zealots who believed they were on the right side of history. When you look at motivation for evil actions, you find a great diversity, but when you look at methods you find remarkable homogeny. Once again, this is how many people wake up one day and realize they have been fighting for the wrong side.

For example, science and academia may be fine things to hang your mental hat on, but on occasion there are studies conducted by legitimate research labs who just coincidentally receive funding from a corporation or activist group that will be impacted by the results of a study. On the principle of mutual exclusivity, this does not necessarily mean that the results of the research are inaccurate, but it is a good place to insert extra skepticism. That skepticism tends to dissolve when the research results give our team an ideological boost. Now "the science" is on our side and we can draw a nice two-dimensional caricature of the other team as ignorant and anti-science. Once again, it may be correct, but being aware of your own willingness to set skepticism aside is important.

By the same token, government agencies and other organizations tend to investigate themselves when a scandal breaks out. Is it surprising when they discover that there was no wrongdoing? Maybe they even went through the trouble to get the most highly esteemed portion of their organization to do the work. How can anyone continue to point fingers once that report comes out? Nothing to see here.

The logic may look like this:

- My team appeared to be guilty of something very embarrassing.

- My team is made up of the "good guys." They wouldn't really do that, or if they did, they could be trusted to root out the problem for the good of the team.

- My team determined that it was all a lie.

- It was all a lie

- Even if it wasn't a lie, it does not matter, because my team winning prevents all the terrible things that will happen if the other team wins.

This is how many people wake up one day, see or hear one thing too many, and suddenly, to their horror, realize they've been fighting for the wrong side for years.

There is nothing wrong with having strong ideological and religious beliefs. Chances are you have very good reason and a lifetime of experience which created and affirmed those beliefs. If there is a moral to the story, it might be to worry less about protecting the team for short term esteem and worry more about protecting your integrity as a person who wants to look back on a life well-lived.

Apply rigorous standards universally. You do not actually need scientific training or a high IQ to know what these standards are. People come by these standards instinctively, however, those instincts tend to only kick in when looking at those we are critical of. We know exactly what logical inconsistency, group think, manipulation of data, and corruption look like when we focus on the away team. Stand back, be willing to take the inevitable social hit along the way, and demand that you and yours be held to the same degree of skepticism that you hold the "other guys" to.

Speaking of human nature...

HUMAN NATURE: GOOD OR BAD? TIME TO DELVE

Is human nature inherently good or inherently bad? Believe it or not, how you answer this question a great litmus tests for determining religious and political beliefs. Even for those who know very little theology and only occasionally glance at political headlines, there is an innate sense that telling another person what you believe about human nature says something about your views on what some call the Judeo-Christian or Traditional Western worldview.

So long as that is the case, critical thinking must do battle with all the pride and prejudice involved with giving any credibility to "the other side." The other problem with the question of human nature is that, for those who hold that there is some form of afterlife awaiting us, it is more comforting to think that we are all doing okay, that we *are* okay, and that therefore, when we face the afterlife, we and basically everyone else will be okay. Such is a world where people are inherently good.

Human nature is a good start point to approach your own deepest held beliefs and apply some critical thinking. It lacks the toxic levels of emotional fire alarms connected with issues such as guns, sexuality, abortion, etc. and is rarely up for discussion on major news sources or political panel discussions. In other words, our "team" has not generally given us much in terms of party doctrine that we must defend.

As far as Critical Thinking goes, though, you might start with asking, "What do you mean by 'good'?" Because there are two issues here. One, how do we even agree on the definitions of these words? And two, if we evolved from "godless" matter over time, then why do we care? Shouldn't the entire concept be as meaningful to us as it is to a rock, or a flower?

With that, you can see how Critical Thinking can quickly lead into philosophical territory, but critical thinking should be practical. Asking the right questions can help you discover the difference between what you believe and what you actually know. Perhaps they are even the same.

For example, a person may believe that eating a diet as prescribed by a nutritionist will improve their health, increase their lifespan, and enhance the quality of life. A longer healthier life awaits! Meanwhile, that same person rarely eats this way and overtime they simply accept the consequences of choosing to live in opposition to their belief about nutrition. Ultimately, they *know* that what they really want is to enjoy life along the way by eating more decadently. This is the difference between believing something and *actually* believing it. This could also be seen as a conflict of values. Whichever one wins is the one that is *actually* valued.

So, here goes. Try some of these questions regarding your beliefs about human nature.

- Do you lock your house doors, windows, screen doors, and turn on some combination of interior and exterior lights at night?

- Do you keep them locked during the day?

- Do you have passwords and encoding for your email, social media and online financial transactions?

- If you and your child were separated in a crowd, would you worry about the actions of the first person who noticed them alone?

- Do you keep your purse or wallet close to you and near your watchful eye when I public?

- If you park your car at a small shop near your house where only you and your neighbors hang out, do you usually lock your car door?

- Are you generally aware of your surroundings from a physical security standpoint?

- Are you cautious when interacting with salespeople, subordinates, or people asking you for assistance?

These questions could go on and on, but since most people answer "yes" to most if not all of those questions, an alien observer would conclude that regardless of what we say, we certainly *act* as if we know we are surrounded by "bad" people.

You could make the argument that we act this way for the sake of a small percentage of bad people in our communities, but the pervasive habits in securing ourselves and belongings is more consistent with seeing almost everyone (even friends and neighbors) as a potential threat.

Then there is the idea that people only "act bad" if they are poor, or not given an equal share of opportunities and resources. Then again, there is a tendency to also believe that where there is great wealth, there is also great crime. Which goes hand in hand with a general view that the more wealth people have, the less empathetic they become. It is hard to reconcile an idea that poverty causes bad conduct while simultaneously seeing the wealthy as inherently immoral or the root of evil.

How about this: Look up the poorest zip code in the United States and look at the crimes per capita. Then look at the ten poorest. The deeper you look, the harder it is to generalize about poverty and criminality. It could be that we just need easy answers to uncomfortable questions and our "team" has a stake in seeing it one way or another.

Have you noticed the topic is starting to spiral out of control again? The types of questions Critical Thinking introduces often require more mental energy than we have on any given day. The real trick is finding a way that gets right to the heart of the question. Cut off all the slack and all the rabbit trails and get to where the rubber meets the road. In the case of human nature, consider The Box.

THE BOX

You may have seen this moral dilemma played out in a movie but there are a couple of dimensions that are usually overlooked.

In this scenario you will be given a small box with a button on it. If you press the button, you will be granted one "genie-like" wish. It could be wealth, fame, a wonderful singing voice, love, beauty, or even time travel. You name it. If you press it, someone, somewhere will die. It may be a friend, neighbor, relative, or total stranger. It doesn't matter. Someone will die.

Are you willing to literally kill to get ahead? You will definitely commit murder by pressing the button. The interesting thing is that you will have absolute impunity from the law. No one will ever be able to connect you to the death. Now, does that change things? Is your morality about murder suddenly altered in knowing you will get away with it?

Wait, you are a good person. You can be trusted with this decision. You were doing fine and had a plan before this box came into your life, you do not need it. You do not want it. You are a good person. People are inherently good.

Of course, that being the case, make a list of all the people you would be comfortable with having access to that box. Should we just put it downtown by a bus stop? Of course not, but what about your best friend's house? What about a beloved family member? Your neighbor?

The degree to which you are comfortable with anyone having access to such an awful device is a pretty good expression of the degree to which you believe that human nature is inherently good. Consider also that while you may trust yourself to take a deep breath and pass on the box, would you trust yourself to keep passing on the opportunity if the box remained in your possession for the rest of your life. As the trials, hardships, and low moments of life come and go, do you really think you could resist the ever-present temptation?

They are good questions. They may lead you to a find that there is a difference between believing that human nature is inherently good and *actually* believing it.

For your consideration: Perhaps you are still holding out from the discussion due to your commitment to moral relativity. Afterall, lying, cheating, stealing, killing, etc. can be good or necessary under the right circumstances and after all, who's to say what is right? There is nothing wrong with this view. Many people share it. However, here is another question. Do you still feel calmly resigned to moral relativity when someone lies, cheats, steals, or otherwise directs harm toward you? Are your views of politicians and religious leaders you disagree with tempered by never seeing them as immoral, mean, or terrible people?

TURN YOUR DAILY NEWS SOURCE INTO A CRITICAL THINKING LABORATORY

LYING STATISTICS, UNTRUSTWORTHY AUTHORITIES, BROKEN GATEKEEPERS, AND RUINED LIVES – THE TRUE STORY OF SALLY CLARK

There are lies, Damn Lies, and Statistics —Mark Twain

Sally Clark was found guilty in a court of law for the murder of her two infant children circa 1992.

When her first child died, the determination was Sudden Infant Death Syndrome and no further investigation was conducted. The family mourned and continued on. In time, she gave birth to her second child who tragically also died under similar circumstances. While Sudden Infant Death is a reality that keeps many new parents awake at night, it seemed beyond unlikely that one family would experience this tragedy twice. The police proceeded with a homicide investigation.

During the trial, a pediatrician who was also a professor at a medical college was brought in to testify.

NOTE: We now enter that territory where the jury is faced with a person possessing advanced degrees, a prominent teaching position, years of experience, and assumed to have been vetted as an absolute expert for the purposes of a homicide investigation. What is more, this expert testimony is exposed to opposing council. If it holds up in front of the jury, then the perception that it is valid becomes powerful.

The professor testified that not only did this occur twice in one family but in each case, the child was about the same age in weeks. He testified therefore that the odds of this being accidental were about 1 in 73 million. This is a statistical reality that pushed jury perception into the "beyond a reasonable doubt" territory.

Subsequently Sally Clark was found guilty and sentenced to life in prison.

Now, put on your Critical Thinking cap for a moment and see what questions you might have as the defense attorney for Sally Clark. What would you do with that statistic?

Here are some possibilities, one of them is the basis for Sally Clark's release from prison.

If there is a one in 300 million chance of winning the lottery, does that mean that lottery winners generally purchase millions of tickets? What about people who win after buying their first ticket ever? Has anyone ever purchased anything close to 300 million lottery tickets in order to win?

What is the margin of error built into those figures?

What are the odds for women who are both in the same age group and ethnic background as the accused?

Are there genetic factors that come into play? The odds of any woman giving birth to triplets is very small but depending on genetics, it becomes more probable.

Are there any medications taken during or after pregnancy that affect those numbers?

Can there be environmental factors such as mold or bacteria which make this type of death more likely?

Is there a connection between birth weight and probability of sudden infant death?

Each of these questions could lead to any number of interesting findings and at the very least, increase healthy skepticism in the mind of the jury.

At the end, it turns out that there were genetic factors involved. Furthermore, evidence about this connection was deliberate withheld by the prosecution.

In the meantime, a mother who suffered the tragic loss of two infants was publicly vilified as the murderer of her own children and spent time in prison as a result. Even though she was released from prison, she never recovered from the multifold tragedy and demonization she experienced. Approximately four years after prison, she died of an alcohol overdose.

Look what some Critical Thinking can do, and more importantly, look at what placing too much trust in authority, prestigious positions, or the manipulated presentation of scientific data can do.

You *will* have instances in your career in which a Soldier will suffer administrative consequences unfairly. You can be the difference. No matter who testifies to what, no matter what baggage you might have, or how a crime in question hits you on a personal level, no one wins when justice misses the mark.

Put some time between hearing a case and making a decision. Give your brain time to start putting those intuitive doubts and gut instincts forward. The more you practice cynical questioning of everything you hear, the better off you will be.

SOME MORE THOUGHT ABOUT STATISTICS

Ever heard that "8 out of 10 doctors recommend (fill in the blank)"? Okay, doctors of what? English, history, education, etc. That may sound funny, but a PHD is sometimes sufficient to be polled as a "doctor" for marketing purposes.

Did you know that there has been at least one significant instance of a product using such a claim about dentists when the truth was that each dentist picked their top three choices? The marketers reasoned that if their brand was in the top three, then that dentist was "recommending" them. If they asked the dentists point blank, "Which toothpaste do you recommend?" the results for the brand in question would have been closer to 50%.

Never believe a statistic or a poll number unless you are willing to get the original documentation and find out the methodology used.

Here's one. What if you found out that the number of PHDs in your city doubled in the last year? That might have you thinking about various topic such as the local job market, the local economy, political policies, etc. But what if there was only one PHD in your "city" the year before? First, of all "city" was defined to include only a small sector of your metropolitan area and the addition of one more PHD created a perception that something much more significant was happening.

There are so many instances of fraudulently presented statistics ruining people's lives that entire books are devoted to the topic. How many instances would it take before you automatically went into cynical mode every time you saw an "expert", or a statistic drive an important conversation? Considering the damage that can be done to entire populations by these instances you may consider a low threshold.

Some people *are* experts and honest brokers, but even experts have agendas. Don't trust any statistics or expert testimony. If it matters, then do the research. There is always one more question or angle to be leveraged against any testimony or evidence.

ON TO THE NEWS

The point of the first two segments in this chapter was to consider certain elements that we are faced with when watching the news source of our choice. We are faced with experts, statistics, authoritative tones, and people who look right at us (the camera) and pierce our souls with their professionally honed expressions of deeply held convictions. So, let's be professionally cynical and recognize that when it comes to stage magic, the magic is necessarily staged.

From the first time something resembling a news story was published, there have been people trying to figure out how to determine the truth of those stories. Generally, there is a certain consensus about getting information from competing sources. Harry S. Truman had multiple newspapers delivered to his door so that he could compare narrative style and facts between the different editing rooms. There is absolutely nothing new about distrust in media and people whose lives intersect with the media proclaiming how venomous the industry can be.

The idea of reading more than one perspective on any event can be very enlightening. When it comes to gathering data, it would be a little naïve to think that one source is sufficient if there is only so much time and space that can be granted to any given story from any one source. However, let's make a game of it and propose a different hypothesis: You can determine if a news story is less than accurate with just critical thinking and nothing else.

Whether or not you agree or disagree with the story is irrelevant. Our *feelings* about a story and the *facts* surrounding that story can be mutually exclusive.

Here are some things to consider for our game. Note the word "consider" in that sentence. The author does not know what news sources you rely on or any of the issues that you move you to act. Let us be professionally cynical and *consider* the following.

- News is a business. It is a business just like coffee shops, fast food, and sporting goods. The goal is profitability. Profitability comes from viewers. No viewers means going broke. More on this later.

- Doctors, nurses, and teachers worry about losing their license. Lawyers worry about being disbarred. Investment brokers worry about crossing the SEC. Scientists face peer review and can lose key positions and grants if they create faulty data. Many professions take oaths, face strenuous examination processes, and live under constant threat of review boards ending their careers or perhaps sentencing them to heavy fines and jail. Journalists do not fall into any of these categories. They either produce economically viable content, or they don't. It's business. The consequences for going so far as to completely fabricate content only extend to financial losses *if* it the fabrication is discovered.

- Journalism as we know it is comprised of news casters who are household names, operate in front of a TV camera, make substantial salaries, interact with the rich and famous, and get to drive the national conversation on every topic. Whatever perception you may have of the things people will do to be in a movie or launch a music career (obtain fame, influence, and wealth) should apply equally to journalism. The same thing goes for the things people do to stay on top once they get there, regardless of profession.

- Almost everyone finds it difficult to look you in the eye and lie to you. We are very good sensors of small facial and body language indicators. That is the gift of nature. People vary but looking another person straight on with a calm unflinching demeanor while lying is almost impossible to pull off. Combine this with a strangely natural inclination to think that others speak to us with an implied honesty in both personal and professional conversations. If someone is standing a few feet from us and looking us square in the face, we feel confident that we are getting the straight story. When we watch our monitors or phones, we see a person looking at us from a perceived arms reach (framing) and they are looking at us dead on when they speak. However, they are actually looking at an inanimate object (a camera) which is usually obscured in the shadows behind the wall of stage lighting. If need be, even an honest person could look directly at a table lamp, book, or vase and comfortably tell a lie without any hint of deception. Our minds have a difficult time detecting the difference between what looks to be a personal interaction with another person in our living space and the actual cold reality of the situation. No matter how you look at it, there is an imbalance between what *we* see (a news anchor looking straight at us) and what *they* see (a lifeless camera lens).

ANGER CAN BE ADDICTING

One of the principles of this book is to recognize that emotions are incredibly powerful mechanisms which can easily overrule every other process in our minds. Once a strong emotion is committed to a person or a topic, there will be a long road ahead for seeing another point of view. How much more so for anger?

There is a robust amount of research and publication on the addictive nature of anger. In the most primitive aspect, it can make you feel alive, in control, strong, ready to take action, confident, and there are even endorphins associated with impulsive anger. Sometimes when someone says they are "passionate" about something, it can also mean that they have a good amount of anger directed at opposition or disregard for their passion project. Imagine a drug that can give you confidence, courage, a sense of control, a sense of purpose, and passion.

Of course, you do not need to look far to see that personal and professional ruin, broken relationships, and stress related illnesses follow in the wake of such a drug. Nonetheless, much like that cup of coffee that is a part of your morning routine or your daily drive, it is hard for many in our media age to imagine going a whole day without a few spikes of righteous anger provided by any number of news stories on our favorite media sources.

Just as the coffee shops know that replacing their various coffee flavors with club soda spritzers will kill their bottom line, so too do news media outlets understand the fiscal benefits of rage.

Peace Sells, But Whose Buying?

Quick question: You check your social media feed and see a cute picture of your neighbor's dog right next to a political story happening in your state that instantly enrages you. Which one will you spend the most time thinking about, reacting to, sharing, bringing up with your closest family and friends, remembering a week from now, etc.?

If the answer for most people was that they will ignore acting on posts about enraging politics in favor of totally engaging in cute animals, then CNN, FOX, MSNBC, etc. would start to resemble a non-stop stream of viral cat videos with commentary. The reality is that anger equals online engagement (likes, shares, etc.) and as any social media mogul will tell you, that is where the money is. Sure, there are plenty of sites that make good money off cute animals, but the full psychological engagement of their audience compared to political anger is rare. What is more, no one is going to attain political power or alter legislative history off the back of pushing cute animals on an audience. News anger is fuel for political power.

Content that makes you angry draws you in, keeps you there, and keeps you tuning in or updating your screen endlessly. Then you get involved in a debate in the comment section and the effect is tenfold. At that point, it does not matter if the story is true or completely fabricated, your primary draw becomes dealing with people who see the world in such a way that you *must* act. If you cannot change their minds, then at the very least, you must work to keep such people from ever being in charge.

This is where existential thinking enters in to turn all evidence in the world around you into a death spiral of confirmation bias and self-fulfilling prophecies. All wrapped in a bow that says the world will literally come to an end if the problem is not fixed.

Considering this, does knowing that provoking you to anger means dollars for someone you don't know change the way you might approach media? Afterall, when someone taps into your physical or mental energies for profit, you get some sort of salary or wage in return. Perhaps the largest civil suit in the history of the world would provoke some thought about our relationship with media. Just joking of course—that is probably a little ridiculous. But consider some of the following before you continue to let a news source, an issue, a politician, or an issue continue to live rent free in your head.

1.   In a nation of over 325 million people, the odds of at least one of them saying or doing something that enrages you every single day is 100%.
2.   In world where everyone carries a digital camera in their pocket and various public and private security cameras line every street, the odds of you being able to see footage of the person(s) who anger you is almost 100%.

3. Carrying around a device that can provide you with instant access to any information or media site in the world at any time provides you with infinite exposure to the people who do things that anger you and the live footage of them doing it.

4. You are a demographic. Your age, your gender, the region you live in, your occupation, etc. all tell someone exactly how to bait you into rage with a headline or photo. Pushing our buttons by the numbers is practically a science...and a lucrative one as well.

Now, give yourself some credit. No other generation has ever had to learn to live with or reconcile this level of exposure to enraging information. It is almost a miracle that we have not all just strangled each other or suffered massive coronaries or strokes by now. However, there is no getting around the fact that there are things going on which demand your attention and furthermore, demand that you act upon them...or are there? It could be that when Critical Thinking is applied, that much of the enraging things happening out there are really have much ado about nothing.

FEAR AND EXISTENTIAL THREATS

Anger is a big draw when it comes to compelling your attention and bringing you back for more. Another big draw is fear. If the hurricane, tornado, wildfire, etc. is anywhere near your zip code, then you will be paying close attention to news sources during that time. When you are worried about something, you want information. You want the latest. Is it over? Is it safe now?

The trouble with genuine fear-inducing events is that they are rare, generally localized and short-term. If people are going to tune in and engage (and get angry), then existential dread needs to be applied to as many aspects of the news cycle as possible.

One thing to think about is death tolls and the overall threat to life that any one topic represents. The major health threat of 2020 is obvious, and yet there is not a single facet of that topic which can be reasonably discussed across the political aisle. Hence, we will chalk that one up as well understood and too polarizing for discussion in this context. However, there is a tendency for various life or death issues to rise and fall within the public's attention span. Various social ills will rise to the top, people will take sides, and many are convinced that we are approaching a critical mass or existential threat "if nothing is done..."

For example, one area that is easy to research is the difference between the frequency of violent crime in the United States and the perception of violent crime. You also need to consider that many statutes are rewritten by legislators in order to broaden the definition of a crime. Something that may not have been an "assault" in 2015 is now categorized as an assault in 2020. Even then, the trend of violent crime in

America is downward. In other words, violent crime is generally less and less of a problem as the years go on. Note the word "generally," much like the stock market, there are sharp bears and bulls, but the overall trend is one direction.

However, when you compare the actual violent crime trends with perceptions generated by polls, there is rarely a year in which perception matched reality. Regardless of which source you go to, you will see that there are years where the incidents of violent crime were low, but perception was at or near an all-time high. How did that disparity occur? The frequency and depth of any issue, regardless of how accurately the facts are presented, has an impact all its own.

While roughly 20 to 30 people are killed by lightening each year in the united states imagine a new cycle in which lightning strikes and injuries are the focus of a national debate for more than one week. At the end of that week about 50% of people would be afraid to go outside on a cloudy day and the other half would be walking around with lightning rods to prove that there is no real threat. Either way, the general sense of importance that lightning strikes should have in our collective minds would be greatly skewed.

When it comes to public health threats and the things we worry about, how much do our concerns and statistical realities match up? Consider the following when contemplating any "everyone is dying from…" type of issue.

According to the CDC...No, wait. What do you believe are the top three causes of death in America? Think of a hot news topic (outside of viruses) that should result in noteworthy death counts and where do you think it falls in the top ten?

Depending on what year you are looking at, the top ten causes of death in the United States looks like this (taken from CDC 2019 statistics):

1. Heart disease: 659,041
2. Cancer: 599,601
3. Accidents (unintentional injuries): 173,040
4. Chronic lower respiratory diseases: 156,979
5. Stroke (cerebrovascular diseases): 150,005
6. Alzheimer's disease: 121,499
7. Diabetes: 87,647
8. Nephritis, nephrotic syndrome, and nephrosis: 51,565
9. Influenza and pneumonia: 49,783
10. Intentional self-harm (suicide): 47,511

Did that match your expectations, more or less? In terms of actual numbers, are you surprised by some of those? Do you believe that the amount of attention for the top five is adequate in the average news cycles?

You can go in and start to sort out the data by age, gender, race, etc. and start to find out those things which you or anyone else should statistically be most concerned with. When you are presented with a "if we don't __, then everyone will die." Or "This is the number one threat to _____" type of story, always go back and get some perspective from the data.

Existential Threats

The word "existential" gets thrown around a bit, but in case you are unaware of what constitutes an actual existential threat, think along the lines of a hostile alien invasion, nuclear war, mass infertility, or a pandemic that kills a majority of those who catch it.

However, the more existential political issues become, the more you will be engaged in the news cycle (and the more potential for anger). How many times have you heard something like, "Everyone will lose their freedom to _____, there will be mass deaths/poverty/starvation....the country as we know it will come to end....the stock market will crash...war is inevitable...the middle east will fall apart....**IF**

- "Our team" loses
- The "other team" gets to choose the next supreme court justice
- The new legislation passes/fails
- "We lose" or "they gain" another senate seat or governorship or second term in the White House
- Etc. etc. etc.

In other words, *everything* is lost unless there is a certain political outcome in the near future. Existential crises equals hysteria, anger, skewed perspectives, irrational behavior, etc.

So, when you feel yourself reacting to an existential threat, just ask yourself if it is really all that existential. If you've lived long enough to be interested in this topic, you lived long enough to have had "your team" lose many battles, elections, supreme court picks, legislative battles, etc. and did that "end of the world" scenario actually happen?

Really go back and find some of the hysteria and rhetoric that preceded a major national political event and then compare how the world actually panned out in the aftermath. In almost every case, the reality was probably no change to your personal status quo. At the very least, it is probably not talked about anymore because the impact was so negligible that it just never comes up.

Remember Y2K? The longer you live, the more Y2K events you will have to endure. Be ready but guard your emotions and thereby your well-being.

THINGS TO CONSIDER WHEN YOU ENGAGE YOUR TRUSTED MEDIA SOURCES.

Note that the title of this section deals with "trusted media sources." This is because you do not need any help or reminders about how to consume or think about those sources that you do not trust and even despise. When it comes those, you are an expert in critical, cautious, and cynical thinking. In other words, and once again, know how to think critically comes naturally. The only barrier is trust. Once someone or something achieves the status of "trusted" in your mind, all the firewalls come down and the front door is unlocked and wide open. To a great extent, "sex sells" works off of this same principle. Advertisers know that advertising puts defenses up in people's minds, but beauty has a way of communicating trust. Somehow, we see beauty and we are more likely to trust. Never hurts to have attractive news anchors, does it?

Imagine that you are like the jury in the Sally Clark trial. The issues at hand are life and death. . As to *all* the data about the case, well, you just do not know. You only know what data enters the courtroom. Experts with amazing resumes give confident testimonies and answer tough questions. There are photos, testimonies from multiple people, opinions provided by opposing sides, and on and on. It seems like you see everything you need to in order to conclude beyond a reasonable doubt. The sad truth is that you really have no way of knowing whether there is critical information that never made it in. What is more, you get the impression that anything left out was either left out because it was unimportant or wouldn't change your mind anyway.

Yet, every year a startling number of innocent people are found guilty of crimes they did not commit, and every year people are released from prison when new evidence emerges to vindicate them. It is said that our legal system is the worst legal system except for all others. Which is just a cynical way of saying that all human enterprises are burdened by human shortfalls. No matter how good you make the system, people will fail or pursue their own agenda without regard to any sense of right and wrong or actual justice.

Consider, as you sit in the information courtroom of your mind, that you do not know what you do not know. Consider that many people who look guilty beyond a reasonable doubt today will be completely vindicated later. Consider that you may be willing to "sentence someone to death" today and then later feel the guilt of knowing you condemned them unjustly. Keeping the masses mostly on one side of an issue or the other is a game of the highest stakes with great profit and untold access to power and control attached to them.

Take haste with hasty headlines.

APPLIED CRITICAL THINKING

Let's try and have a little fun with another practical exercise. The following scenario will look familiar in form but will lack any of the actual issues of our world. While it may be more effective to find an *actual* news story and analyze it in the context of this book, doing so invokes your current political beliefs and subsequent emotional investments. Hence, real reporting techniques will combine with fake issues for arguments sake.

SCENARIO: You are watching a segment about the lack of bowls full of fresh water for dogs on public streets. The media you subscribe to reflects your view that federal legislation is needed to ensure that all commercial sites keep bowls of cold, fresh water outside their doors for stray and domestic dogs. Senator Canis Lupus is the Senator you support and is on-air facing off against Senator Felix who says dogs already get all the support they need without this new legislation. Your host (your *favorite* TV news host) is Ms. Nicely, and she oversees the discussion.

NICELY: Okay, well we all know the issue so let's go ahead and get things going. I'll start with you, Senator Felix. Your hardline opposition to this legislation flies right in the face of an overwhelming majority of Americans who support it. Why the tough stance? And why does your party routinely ignore the needs of dogs?

FELIX: That last statement does not really reflect. I voted ten times to ensure that dogs get vaccinated for rabies and heartworms prior to being adopted.

NICELY: Senator Felix, we're talking about fresh, cold water for dogs—something you oppose.

FELIX: I'm *not* opposed to dogs having cold, fresh water...

NICELY: Your record indicates otherwise. Are you telling me now that you support Senator Lupus' legislation?

FELIX: Look, you're conflating the facts...

LUPUS: Nicely, I just gotta jump in here.

NICELY: Go ahead, Senator Lupus.

LUPUS: The facts are Senator Felix has stood against dogs having access to cold, fresh water for decades. No one here is surprised that you would be happy to see a trail of dead or near dead dehydrated dogs lining every street in American and frankly, I have no idea how you keep getting elected by the good people of your district.

FELIX: Nicely, I want to answer that. It is a complete...

NICELY: Wait your turn Senator. We still need to hear from our five panelists who have joined us in the studio. Please welcome Lassie, Benji, Snoopy, Rex, and America's sweetheart, Lady.

END TRANSCRIPT

Take a moment and mentally list all the problems with this segment. If you are using this for a group exercise, then open for discussion while dissuading any references to actual issues, TV or political personalities, and networks.

The preceding script amounts to about one minute of on-air screen time and yet look how power-packed the shortfalls and deception are layered on. Can you honestly say that this does not resemble any number of heated on-air "debates" you've seen on the news? Remember, the audience for this show is a demographic that overwhelmingly supports Senator Felix. To them, even seeing Senator Felix's face raises their blood pressure.

NOTE: The following breakdown is not all inclusive and many other significant points could and should be made.

- Nicely begins with Senator Felix. This establishes a sense that she is being courteous and giving him top billing. As a framing device, it puts Felix in a position to be heard up front, in his own words, and to determine the way in which the discussion will flow. Clearly, Nicely want everyone to know that she is a fair and objective host who is giving someone she disagrees with every possible advantage and courtesy. Of course, within seconds this illusion is broken and yet the alibi remains permanently affixed.

    The viewers are on Nicely's side. They are on her "team" and are subsequently emotionally invested in her and will defend her "decency, professionalism, and objectivity" with such examples giving the opposition the opening statement no matter what. If anything, fans of the show may actually criticize Nicely in this segment for being too fair, or too nice to a Senator that "everyone" knows is wrong and detestable.

- In reality, Nicely does not give Senator Felix the opening, nor does she allow him to frame the discussion. Instead, she does something called Poisoning the Well. With just one simple, quick sentence or two, Senator Felix is already in the hole and fighting an uphill fight. His introduction steals any advantage that speaking first should have provided. Let's take a look:

Your hardline opposition to this legislation flies right in the face of an overwhelming majority of Americans who support it. Why the tough stance? And why does your party routinely ignore the needs of dogs.

- "Hardline opposition" – Hardline is an opinion (not a fact) but denotes that Felix's position is not reasonable or moderate. Furthermore, opposition is usually another way of saying that someone supports an opposing idea. However, since "opposition" is a negative word, it is more effective and in this case, it magnifies "hardline."

Second, we are told that an "overwhelming majority of Americans" support the thing that Felix opposes. This puts Felix into an even more radical and out of touch hole that he must dig his way out of. The segment might as well have ended there.

Then comes the moralistic condemnation, "Why the tough stance?" Yes, how dare he? Thank goodness our hero is here to speak for us and put him in his place. If you really are watching at home, your body is already providing the body chemistry of a stress response to your environment. Hopefully, the kids or your significant other don't need anything important from you in the next few minutes.

- Is it really an overwhelming majority who support the legislation? What does that even mean? Nicely says it with firm, swift authority and certainty. She does not cite a poll or specific numbers. Oftentimes news agencies conduct their own poll prior to a segment which circulates among their own viewers. What would you expect such a poll to reveal?

Perhaps the poll was conducted by a third party that both sides generally trust but it was conducted among children, or only among dog owners. The poll could be years old before this story became a national issue. There could be several polls which all contradict each other. The methodology and questions asked could also guarantee one result.

You are led to believe that the poll reads something like, "Do you support legislation to provide cold, fresh drinking water for dogs outside of all businesses?" But the poll question could have been, "Do you believe that someone should care for stray dogs?" or, "Do you like to see dogs in public?" or even, "Do you like dogs?" You might be startled at the methodology of some polls used in such debates.

Perhaps the results were a three-way split with a slight majority in favor. This too could be presented as an "overwhelming" majority as plurality results sometimes are.

However, the dynamic that is really at work is the fact that viewers like and support Nicely. They will assume that "a majority" really does feel as strongly as they do, and also that Nicely would never say something misleading or false on air.

And why does your party routinely ignore the needs of dogs?

- That is nasty stuff, and the segment is only three sentences deep. The preceding statement continues to poison the well and introduces the idea that Felix is inhumane and part of a system of inhumanity toward at least one part of the animal kingdom. Such a statement also fits into something called a Red Herring. In other words, an entirely different, emotionally charged, and mostly unrelated issue just thrown in right before Felix responds. It is a categorical statement that brings in dozens of complex debates and activities over decades and pronounces unqualified judgement. The only thing more certain could be gravity itself. All that is to say that this statement is also a Strawman tactic in which an opponent is qualified as a moral villain or part of a villainous group in order to invalidate their views and goals.

There is tremendous power in this statement alone and it derails both Felix and the entire segment. Once again, the discussion is over before it begins. Felix and his supporters may be able to provide volumes of data, occurrences, and talking points to dispute such a statement, but the power of emotional support for Nicely and her "tough, unapologetic" tone against Senator Felix will override any questions or objections that should otherwise have been a red flag.

Does Felix's party "routinely" ignore the needs of dogs? How? When? Is it unilateral or are there times where they genuinely supported dogs? What do dog owners who support Felix think? You can bet that around 50% of dog owners in this fictional world would support Felix and also resent Nicely's comment.

If you are Felix, your head is likely going a hundred miles an hour and you are more than a little bit incensed. Good news is it is now your turn (sort of).

FELIX: That last statement does not really reflect, look, I voted ten times to ensure that dogs get vaccinated for rabies and heartworms prior to being adopted.

NICELY: Senator Felix, we're talking about fresh, cold water for dogs, something you oppose.

- Of course, Senator Felix began by addressing the accusatory jab which Nicely inserted before handing the discussion to him. This is a trap which allows Nicely to interrupt him because he is "avoiding the question." She would then contend that she was doing her job by keeping him from getting off topic. In other words, she hit Felix with an unqualified accusation as a red herring and then when Felix defends himself against the accusation, that defense is treated as a red hearing itself.

Once again, emotional support for Nicely keeps the viewers from understanding this tactic and firmly entrenched in the idea that Nicely is really holding Felix accountable. Also, it looks like since Felix may be scoring some points and inserting doubt into the minds of Nicely's audience about his villainy. Good time to interrupt and pile on more accusation.

Therefore, Nicely interrupts and demands "getting back on topic." However, we go from talking about the role of federal legislation to the very concept of whether dogs should have cold, fresh water. This is conflating and confusing. The goal is to stop Felix from making a good point about his character and his intentions and replace it with a conflated idea that opposing federal legislation is equal to opposing dogs' access to water. Now, Felix is twice the villain he was before and stuffed with even more straw in his strawman costume.

What kind of monster wants to keep dogs from drinkable water?

Now, quick break to point something out. One of the biggest problems when it comes to Critical Thinking and the news is *pacing*. Discussions and tactics go very fast. You may notice that these individuals speak at a rate that is two or three times faster than your own conversational tone.

By the time your brain has a chance to contemplate a dubious statement, you have already had to absorb three or four more such statements, and then on and on and on. The entire process is a steamroller that is designed to flatten your better judgement and join in on a mob mentality.

Something inside you starts shouting like you are at a sporting event. "Yeah, go, go! You get him! What? No way! Get him! Get him!" There may be little separation between how you feel during a news "debate," and a professional boxing match. The entire setup hinges on your unqualified investment in the host and network along with a willingness to let the opposition get screwed over by the process. However, while enjoying a boxing match, you know that you are feeding your "lizard brain." By contrast, you might fool yourself into believing that a news segment like this one is highly intellectual.

It really does take several pages of dissecting text to analyze and contemplate any given minute or two of national news coverage or even online content. It is no wonder that everyone feels run over by the current media culture.

Now, on with the show.

FELIX: I'm not opposed to dogs having cold, fresh water…

NICELY: Your record indicates otherwise. Are you telling me now that you support Senator Lupus' legislation?

- Senator Felix is once again on his back heels trying to respond to Red-herring strawman accusations which are immediately interrupted. It is as if his being allowed to complete a sentence might endanger the momentum of the segment and detract from Nicely's overall goals.

  When Nicely interrupts, she maintains the conflated idea that Felix is opposed to dogs having access to water by emphasizing that Felix's record proves otherwise. Imagine an elected official with a proven legislative record of opposing dogs being allowed to drink water. Once again, as long as Nicely keeps hammering Felix, the audience stays tuned and stays angry. You can almost hear people yelling at their TV screens, "What kind of monster is this guy?!"

  Now look at how Nicely contrasts her first sentence with the question, "Are you telling me that you now support?…"

By this point, the average viewer is now fully convinced that opposition to the legislation is opposition to dogs having access to drinking water. Afterall, if you are not opposed to dogs drinking water, then you must support the legislation. Right? Aren't they moral equivalents? No. However, within 24 hours of this broadcast every discussion on this topic from watercoolers to Capitol Hill will revolve around the certainty that those who oppose the bill simply do not want dogs to have drinking water and are evil people.

It is possible that you can both oppose this bill and love dogs.

Next Segment:

FELIX: Look, you're conflating the facts...

LUPUS: Nicely, I just gotta jump In here.

NICELY: Go ahead, Senator Lupus.

LUPUS: Now, the FACTS ARE Senator Felix, that you have stood against dogs having access to cold, fresh water for decades. No one here is surprised that you would be happy to see a trail of dead or near dead dehydrated dogs lining every street in American and frankly, I have no idea how you keep getting elected by the good people of your district.

- Senator Felix remains on the defensive, which is an inherently weak place to be—looking guilty of something. Engineering discourse so that your opponent must begin on the defensive and remain there is effective, but also a disservice to Critical Thinking and fact finding.

Felix is then interrupted again, which makes it three for three. Fans of the show would retain the impression that Felix was given a fair shot and refused to stay on topic, distracting viewers with accusations.

Here Senator Lupus kindly asks for permission to join in. His tone is such that he is a reasonable and civil individual who is clearly compelled by moral necessity to join in. Nicely, being able to protect Felix's right to finish a sentence, let Lupus take over.

Lupus states that Felix has been opposed to dogs having drinking water for decades and that Felix would be happy to see dead or suffering dogs all over America. Does Felix really have decades of policy decisions and statements in which he shows contempt for dogs drinking water? Do we really believe that there is someone out there who wants to drive around looking at suffering animals? What difference does it make? Lupus' tone is clear, and the viewers want him to pile on Felix.

It all sounds like pure hubris, and you should be asking questions or demanding proof, but if you oppose Felix, then emotionally you are good with what is happening.

Lupus also engages in the fallacy of mind-reading as if anyone can know what Felix is thinking or what motivates. Note also that Lupus is not speaking toward the content of his legislation or bringing up any pertinent facts regarding economic impact or statistical needs. He is simply piling on with Ad Hominem attacks against Felix. Was that really a morally strong impetus to "jump into" the conversation early?

Lupus then doubles down on the idea that a "majority" of people are opposed to Felix's views by calling Felix's constituents good people who will probably stop supporting him. By this token, Felix is out of touch and basically evil. Strange how nothing of substance regarding the issue has come up yet.

FELIX: Nicely, I want to answer that. It is a complete...

NICELY: Wait your turn Senator. We still need to hear from our five panelists who have joined us in the studio. Please welcome Lassie, Benji, Snoopy, Rex, and America's sweetheart, Lady.

- Here comes the finale. Felix attempted to assert his defense again as the accusations against him grow more bold and disturbing. This is followed by one more interruption before he can complete a sentence. Nicely then lets us know that Felix will no longer be contending with just herself and Senator Lupus, but also with five more panelists who are passionately on the pro-water bowl side of the issue. To make matters worse, one of the panelists is a beloved celebrity. Senator Felix would have to be a real jerk to speak sternly to Lady. But then again, Felix is already a jerk because he is on the opposite side of someone as wonderful, loveable, and socially accepted as Lady. Fans of Nicely would applaud this fair and equitable treatment of the issue and they would believe that since Felix is so wrong and detestable as a human being, that it is good and necessary to see so many brave voices come out against him and put him in his place on live television. "Thank goodness for Lady...I just love her."

Don't forget that stacking several proponents of an issue against one representative of the opposition solidifies the idea that "everyone" knows that the "other guy" is wrong and represents a tiny minority.

With that, let's go back to lessons learned from the Sally Clarke trial. The big difference between the trial of Senator Felix and the Trial of Sally Clarke is that Sally Clarke had a representative who was given due time to present a case and evidence on her behalf. We have become accustomed to public "courts of opinion" in which the accused is mute while a thousand prosecutors opine for days on end.

In the preceding scenario it was essentially seven against one, which, is not all that uncommon for some news programs.

Putting that aside, let's take the scenario out a few years. The world changes a little bit, and you start to hear and see things from different people. There are a couple of scandals here and there, and you are not quite as trusting of Nicely or anyone else for that matter.

In time, you discover that Senator Felix was a lifelong advocate for getting stray dogs off of the streets and used much of his personal fortune to build some of the best no-kill dog shelters in the country. Felix was also influenced by his own community where a water bowl policy much like the one proposed by Senator Lupus created a rise in stray dogs in busy areas where they were frequently hit by cars, got into violent encounters with pedestrians, and the number of strays doubled in that community. Furthermore, it turns out that Senator Lupus' spouse holds a patent on a type of sanitary water container and dispenser which Lupus' bill mandated as the only type of bowl that could be purchased by businesses.

At this point, you regret ever supporting Senator Lupus and admit that you have seen the adverse effects on the water bowl policy in your own community. You cannot understand why it was possible to watch five hours of news per day for weeks on end as the topic was discussed and *never* heard about Senator Felix's true background or the reasons why he opposed Lupus. How is it possible that none of the most important talking points ever came to light? How indeed?

CONCLUSION

Hopefully, you were able to see through some of the silliness of the dog bowl debate and recognize some similarities in the real world of modern media. The logical fallacies, distractions, and character assassinations are easy to detect when targeted at your team. When our viewpoints are coddled by our chosen media who misrepresent and shut out the other team, it is difficult to know what you don't know.

If you are watching news-related content and feel your adrenaline rushing or blood pressure rising, try turning it off and asking some questions about what you are looking at. Do those accusation make sense? Is that sensationalistic? Is there really such a clear connection between supporting one side of an issue and moral character? Is it possible to have the same values and support different solutions?

Lastly, do not forget to consider that when you keep your eyes, attention, thoughts, and energy focused on the outrage of the day, then you are essentially working for the media outlets who provide the content and are putting money in their pocket. If they are going to profit from your attention and emotions, make them earn it.

WARFIGHTING AND THE WAR WITHIN

WARFIGHTING AND COGNITIVE GROOMING

What you will read shortly is not an insult directed against the military or anyone serving in the military. Instead, it is a recognition of what the military does (warfighting) and what warfighting as a business model necessarily means for business as usual.

The military does not require or reward Critical Thinking. As a result, the more time you spend achieving success in the military, the more often you go without experiencing or even witnessing deliberate Critical Thinking as a part of daily operations.

No?

Here are three words: Memorization, Motivation, and Compliance.

Success in the military revolves around those three centers of gravity more than any other factor. Promotion boards resemble intensive Jeopardy sessions in which participants must demonstrate by chapter and verse a broad-based of knowledge memorized by rote. This is the preeminence of knowledge, which *is* a hallmark of army cognitive conditioning. Smart leaders are veritable warehouses of knowledge. But there is a big difference between being Google (an infinite reach into all available knowledge) and being Deep Blue (a computer that *applied* knowledge in simulated Critical Thinking to defeat the world's foremost chess champion). Outside of this, there is an endless appreciation for showing high levels of motivation.

Training in METL tasks, annual compliance requirements, and even most military schools that support promotion requirements revolve around repetition, muscle memory, and information via "firehose." You can "click-through" all instructional content and then take a multiple-choice test using best guess to score 70% or above. Scored below 70%? Just retake it until you get there. The "Boggle playing chicken" from *King of the Hill* could pass all of these tests under the standard conditions.

This is not how you generate a population of seasoned, Critical Thinking leaders. Yet, it *is* how you create a population of warfighters that all "sing from the same sheet of music, speak the same language, share strict standards, ethics, and employ identical methods of getting any job done." The result is a uniform force that is easy to maneuver, supply, task, and hold accountable. This is how you win wars.

Wars are won by small groups who can receive streamlined orders, move out with high levels of motivation, and aggressively get to the next objective. *Message to Garcia,* anyone?

While there are times to question orders or object to a course of action, such times are woven discretely into MDMP and closed-door discussions. In the case of MDMP, it is often not conducted in-depth or sometimes not at all. As far as closed-door sessions, depending on command climate, they are generally cautious, brief, and perhaps dangerous to a young leader's career. Barring the refusal of anything unethical, illegal, or immoral, you might get in a clarifying question or two, and then you know it is time to start moving out as if the order you just questioned came from your own mind.

There is one significant exception to the necessary marginalization of critical thought in the military, and that is what the Army calls Army Design Methodology or ADM. Design Methodology does not revolve around answering questions as much as it revolves around getting as many diverse points of view in a room, removing ranks and protocols, and then openly contemplating whether we are even asking the *right* questions. In this environment, a PFC's viewpoint is on equal footing with any idea from a Colonel. Now *that* is Critical Thinking.

Honestly, though, how often have you ever been brought in for some intensive ADM?

Nonetheless, you are a **leader**, and even the military acknowledges that a leader must conduct a self-inventory of strengths and weaknesses. It may be pertinent to recognize that, even as an intelligent person, your success in the rank structure could also be the very cause of needing to move "critical thinking" into the "improve" category. Thus far, you have been trained to operate in a particular sphere of cognitive operations. It gets the mission done. But since we've been looking at intellectual hazards of warfighting, let's switch to contemplating the war within

THE WAR WITHIN

The war within in this context is not about dealing with PTSD or overcoming doubts and ethical dilemmas. It is about the reason why Critical Thinking is so rare and so difficult to master. To think critically, you must defeat your pride, most sacred beliefs, your experiences, likes, dislikes, emotions, pride (yes, mentioned twice), goals, you name it. Pretty much everything that makes you at any given moment is in your way if you want to think critically.

Here's why.

Everything life has taught you thus far has given you a distinct sense of how any given problem is *supposed to be* solved. Maybe you've heard that in the mind of a hammer, every problem is a nail. It may be a crude way to look at it, but we are all hammers in our own way. Surgeons, computer scientists, theoretical physicists, and expert code breakers are all in the business of applying intellect to solve problems. But each field will groom different approaches to problems based on the nature of the work.

Though cited in various publications, there is an urban legend that seems to have no definitive origin. It goes something like this:

A delivery truck mistakenly ran into a low bridge with such force that recovery crews could not push, pull, drag, or cut the mass from under the bridge. Traffic began to pile up, and a young girl who was tired of waiting rolled down her window and yelled, "Why don't you just let all the air out of the tires?" Shortly after that, the truck was pulled out of the scene.

Depending on how the story is told, it is easy to sharp-shoot it, but the reason the story stays around is because of the point it makes. We become experts of sorts and apply our specific mastery of knowledge to problems at hand, which then blinds us to more obvious solutions that the open mind of a child could see immediately.

Here are a couple more examples of this type of out-of-the-box solution that you may be familiar with.

Alexander the Great and the Gordion Knot: Alexander the Great seemed blessed by every conceivable form of leadership genius. This included, at least according to legend, an open mind when it came to problem-solving. As the legend goes, an impossible knot woven in commemoration of a previously fulfilled prophecy would only be unwoven by a person destined to rule all of Asia. There are two versions of how Alexander defeated the knot and sealed his destiny.

The first version states that he simply drew a sword and cut it clean through. The second (and more likely) version asserts that he undid the pole from its setting pin, slipped the knot from the pole's now open bottom and used the newfound slack to unravel the rope quickly. In either case, the story has been the standard-bearer of out-of-the-box problem solving for over a thousand years.

People tend to impose rules or barriers on problems that may not exist. In the case of the Gordian Knot, no overt restriction on removing the pin from the from or use of brute force. Whatever fortune teller devised the knot probably knew that a true conqueror would not accept status quo barriers between themselves and future glory.

Another take on this story was seen in Marvel's *Captain America: The First Avenger*. During a military training montage, the troops were in the middle of what looked like a 20-mile forced march and given the option to ride back in the jeep if they could capture the flag from a nearby flag pole. The exhausted troops all tried and failed miserably as the drill instructor let them know that "no one has captured that flag in 15 years." Then, just as everyone gave up, the puny recruit who would one day be Captain America simply walked up to the flagpole, undid the pin, let the pole fall to the ground, and removed the flag.

This is where the worn-out notions of "outside the box" enter into corporate lingo and motivational seminars. We use this to cultivate our methods of getting out of our respective boxes. The fact that this concept is now seen as something trite means we should call it something else. How about *lateral thinking? Free thinking? Open-mindedness?* You decide.

Okay, with all that being said, let's have a little bit of fun. Learning through playing and games is the most natural way any advanced organism learns. Watching dogs, foxes, or wolves, you might even speculate that they are always at play, even when hunting, fighting, and marking their territory. Exploration and discovery at the heart of play and these are open-minded pursuits.

Without any further hesitation. Here are the rules of the game. You need to connect the nine given dots by utilizing four straight lines. Each line will start where the last line ended. Just to clarify, here is an example that follows the rules but does not get the solution.

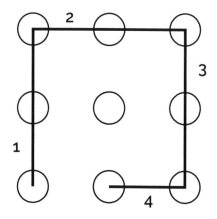

Now, review the rules and give it a try.

Solution on the next page

Okay, so here it is.

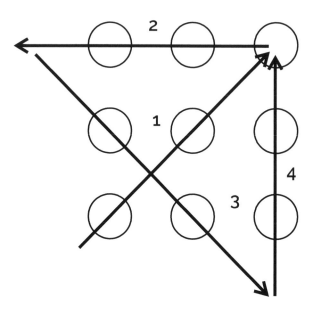

For reference, here are the dots by themselves. Go ahead and draw the solution on top of them.

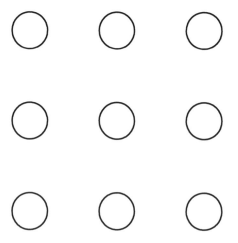

What did you notice?

Time to talk about what just happened because this is just one of those perfect illustrative moments. First, if you observe the configuration of the dots, it creates a literal box. The solution is only possible if you draw "outside the box."

However, look at everything that happened in the last few pages. This text has been your guide, and therefore it represents any source of information you consume, trust, or utilize for educational purposes. Take note. The author can determine how you will see a problem and restrict your ability to find a solution. In other words, this problem was set up in such a way to deliberately keep you "in the box," but it was done deceptively through structure.

Go back to the page where this dot problem was introduced and look at what is shone immediately after the instructions. It looked just like this.

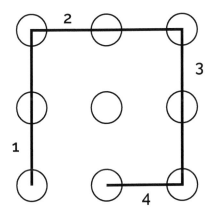

Isn't that interesting? The purpose of that diagram was to help you understand the game's rules with a visual example. How helpful. False. What happened was a diagram reinforced and permeated your natural tendency to work inside the box. In other words, this "helpful clarification" was a deliberate misdirection. It was a visual wolf in sheep's clothing.

What is worse, if push came to shove, there would be an alibi for the author stating that only one paragraph earlier, the importance of going "outside the box" was emphasized. Then, the reader was presented with a box, some clarifying rules, and a solution that simply required going *outside* the box.

What? How can that be wrong?

Welcome to lesson one on the power of trust and ways in which *any* presentation could easily manipulate you into seeing things a certain way, even under the guise of helping you see things for yourself.

How can you trust anything in this book from this point forward? Perfect. Now you are on board. Simple answer: Stay alert, stay alive. Critical Thinkers are alert. Leaders are alert.

You may still be skeptical about the ease with which a text or presentation can box in your perception of a problem or an issue. Fine, there is no way advertisers, journalists, teachers, motivational speakers, and writers can be so sure about how their craft can streamline what their audience perceives.

Unless, of course, there is...

And you will read this last

You will read this first

And then you will read this
Then this one

Interesting.

You had better believe that individuals who make significant salaries creating text for public consumption know this trick, the "box" trick, and plenty of others (think advertisers, media, politicians, directors, speechwriters, etc.). Stay alert.

How does this apply to the war within? Well, in multiple ways, your cultural upbringing, your choices in entertainment, education, information, etc. have created vast matrixes of preconceived ideas about what is and is not possible, what should and should not be happening in any given situation, what types of people might do certain kinds of things, and how certain types of problems should be solved. Our minds are full of boxes.

This is the war within. If you win this war, you can practice Critical Thinking in the same way that you apply a multitude of exact body mechanics to squeeze off a bullseye at the range. However, as is the case with many young Soldiers who spent their childhoods shooting rifles incorrectly, there will likely be as much *un*learning as learning.

THE DOWN AND DIRTY OF THE WAR WITHIN

Time to see part of the battlefield in the war within for what it is: Prejudice, specifically *cognitive prejudice*.

In this day and age, almost every possible belief system, cultural background, or lifestyle preference is more or less politically loaded. As a rule, once *anything* becomes politicized, critical thinking and actual scientific processes become near impossible. So long as any conclusion galvanizes an individual to one side of the political fence or the other, they will either refuse to see or refuse to admit something that would affiliate them with the "wrong side." Part of being human is sensitivity to the consequences of allegiances. It only takes one failure of any number of "litmus test" views to experience hostility, banishment, and isolation.

Still, want to engage in Critical Thinking? Critical Thinking does not seek comfortable or convenient conclusions; it is satisfied only with accurate conclusions.

With that said, time for more self-assessment. Here is a list of words that are important in contemporary (2021-ish) society.

Next to each word is a series of box choices that range from very negative to very positive in nature. If you are not comfortable writing on the page, then simply scan through and make a note of where you would place an "X" on each line as it represents your sentiments on each word in question.

Descriptive Word	😃	🙂	😐	🙁	😠
Politicians					
Scientist					
Libertarian					
Conservative					
Atheist					
Conservation					
Climate Change					
Social Justice					
Male					
LGBTQ					
Liberal					
Female					
Socialism					
Representation					
Non-White					
Censorship					
White					
Oil					

Here is a question. After scanning through this, did you immediately think, "Hey, why did you leave out _____?" If something stood out to you and you had a strong feeling about its absence, then that is the perception inventory in action. Such a reaction perfectly illustrates the connection between your perception of a missing category and emotional connection.

Here is another question. Isn't it interesting that a series of words can (in most cases) be logically inventoried according to emotional reaction graphics? You could add another 100 of the most commonly used words in today's society and find that you have some emotional connection to each and every one of them.

That is how your Critical Thinking gets hi-jacked. As soon as a person is affiliated with just about any belief system or point of view, an entire world of emotional baggage comes between you and objectively handling any issues relating to that person. There is something very primordial about our tendency to drop our fellow humans into "good guy" and "bad guy" affiliations. This is much like team affiliations. We all wear team jerseys of different kinds. If you are military, then that is one jersey. You have a generational jersey, a hometown/state jersey, ideological jerseys, cultural or racial jerseys, hobby or recreational jerseys, *actual* sport team jerseys, and on and on and on. It is almost impossible to look at actions committed by those on "your team" in the same way that you look at those same actions when committed by "the other team."

When it comes down to it, the human mind has found excellent shortcuts for categorizing the billions of bits of information it needs to analyze and connect in any given day (yes, day). Many of those shortcuts are built around friendly and unfriendly groupings of various kinds. You might be utterly indifferent to all sports teams, or you may want to start a literal fight with someone just because of a team they support. We may value some categories of "teams" more than others, but we all have our hot topics.

Self-inventory is essential to recognize where your ability to think critically is most in danger. It does not matter where you stand on any issue or which groups you feel most support; the point is that quick filter settings in your mind could lead you into misjudging, being easily deceived, or taken advantage of. As a leader, your personal life is your own business. Still, when it comes to making judgment calls that affect others' lives, you will either employ objective and critical thinking habits or find yourself on the wrong side of an IG or EO-based complaint. Ultimately, you want to look back on your leadership time and know, really know, that you did not hurt anyone because of preconceived ideas.

EMOTIONS AND FEELINGS: GOOD OR BAD?

The topic at hand is Critical Thinking and getting emotional reactions to the world around us in check. It would seem like we are knocking on the door of "My facts don't care about your feelings." Sentiments such as that are common in the world of political debates, and especially in any of those infamous Christian vs. Atheist sectors of the internet. The rationalistic and scientific approach to reality is closely knit with Critical Thinking, and therefore it would seem as if we should all strive to be ultra-biocomputers.

Not so fast.

Emotions are powerful and an integral part of the human experience. They make life worth living and are essential to meeting some of the challenges of life. Just because you feel an emotion does not mean you are engaged in subjective or irrational thought. Even those who speak loudest about the dangers of emotional or feeling-based beliefs will, themselves, become passionate and animated when doing so.

Seeing someone abuse a loved one will provoke strong emotion. However, that is a rational and justified emotion. You may believe that your neighbor down the street is a jerk because every time you drive by and wave at him, he just gives you a flat stare. For the most part, the negative feelings you develop toward him will be rational and evidence based. We all have associative feelings built around our life experiences.

The gift of Critical Thinking is that your emotions are built around an accurate view of any given situation. Is your neighbor really a jerk? What if, unbeknownst to you on a previous date, a member of your family drove your car, accidentally road up on the curb, and drove over his flowers planted near the street? Suddenly his failure to wave and merely grimace at you driving by seems like a rational response. Under those circumstances, your waving could be seen as cavalier or mocking.

Backing away from emotional connections at the outset of a new situation, asking the right questions, and getting more information *first* is the key to using the powerful energies of thoughts and feelings in a dynamic and life-changing way.

This is some touchy stuff. Let's look at a neutral (if that is possible) and lighthearted example taken from the real world. It is the case of "Wireless iPhone Charging in the Microwave." It is a fun little slice of the past and connects to the fact that a sense of *wonder* is also an easily manipulated emotion. Everyone loves a good magic trick, right? Too often, ill-motivated people take advantage of our best qualities.

IPHONE IN THE MICROWAVE

Pranksters will always be amongst us. We all like to prank each other a little bit from time to time, and at some point, you have started a friendly prank feud with a family member or friend. However, there are people with simply nothing better to do than to see what they can get away with on a national or global scale. Here is what happened.

In 2014, an image that bore an uncanny resemblance to iPhone marketing products started making the rounds on the internet. It claimed that one of the new phone features was the ability to recharge wirelessly in the Microwave.

Bear in mind that the product was called "Wave," and the flyer insinuated that this was because of a connection to this radical new ability to sync with micro-waves.

The text explained that the new phone "contained new drivers that could interface with the device's radio-baseband, allowing it to synchronize with microwave frequencies and use them to recharge the battery." It then specified that one minute and thirty seconds was required to attain a full charge.

First of all, you would be hard-pressed to see too many people admit they fell for this, but once police departments started putting out warnings about the scam, you could assume it was due to some 911 calls related to the topic.

However, let's see how this scam's psychology skirted right past the rational mind of the victims.

- Perfectly counterfeited logos, media style, and language of a trusted brand known for generating "wow factor" leaps of technology? Check.

- Connecting the legitimate name of the new product to a plausible reason that the company would choose that exact name (highlight the singular revolutionary feature)? Check.

- Posting the false information in precisely the places you would expect to find legitimate product information and fake or counterfeited accounts that look legitimate? Check.

- Specific time recommendations as one might expect with any charging instructions? Check.

- Throwing legitimate and technical sounding gibberish at the reader's initial doubts? Check.

- Knowing that curiosity will often kill the cat? Check.

The degree to which you would be fooled or almost fooled by this scam would have not so much to do with how smart you are, but more to do with your biases and emotions connected to the factors at hand:

- Which sources of information you find most trustworthy

- How prone you are to the most starry-eyed views of technology

- How susceptible you are to taking technical gibberish as authoritative or intelligent

- The frame of mind you are in when you see it

- Just how curious or adventurous you are feeling at that moment.

Microwave charging may seem ridiculous, but a close examination of the last ten news stories that got your blood boiling might reveal more than one occasion in which you were similarly taken in. Rage equals "clicks," and clicks equals cash. There are no certifications or licenses at stake when it comes to misleading news text. No hypocritic oaths need to be broken. Information is a market, and the only sin is that which leads to irrelevance. Critical Thinking can open your eyes to many things, including whether someone is worthy of trust and also the degrees people will go to lure others in for fun, power, or profit.

Seriously though, what are some Critical Thinking questions that could have saved people from temptation in this case?

- Cell phones *can* be charged wirelessly, and maybe a microwave could do the job, but isn't the phone case still just glass, metal, and plastic?

- Did anyone mention this feature when I bought my phone?

- Is it listed on the box as one of the features?

- If the product was *named* after a connection to the Microwave, shouldn't that have been part of the entire sales pitch that led me to buy the phone?

- Have I heard anyone talk about this or seen any of my friends put a cell phone in the microwave?

Even without much experience in the technological world, the questions above would seem to come pretty naturally to anyone who stepped back and took a moment to contemplate it.

So long as you possess strong emotional reactions to certain people and ideas, you could easily be led past multiple logical speed bumps and stop signs into more ridiculous claims than microwave-intelligent phone charging. Once again, considering is not viewing emotional connections as a weakness but validating emotional connections as a habitual strength.

Now that this book has engaged in some mental conditioning regarding logical fallacies that kill Critical Thinking, let's look at a formalized list.

RESPECT THE PROCESS

RESPECT THE PROCESS PART 1: DEFEATING THE ENEMY-WITHIN

If you are reading this, you most likely have enough time in service to be somewhat cynical about Army methods. Yet, if you are inclined to see things this way, then you also have enough time in service to recognize the difference between a mission statement and the commander's intent. As a leader, you can do wonders when you know the basic thing that the boss is trying to get done as opposed to an exact prescription on how to do it. The same thing will happen when you take a moment to realize the intent of MDMP before diving into the mechanics. Understanding this intent will also help you understand and convey (at least some) respect for the process. By the way, MDMP will not only produce better mission statements for Soldiers, but also better statements of intent (See Chapter 5).

Thus far, this chapter introduced a few things that dominate MDMP: Developing a Course of Action; producing an OPORD; making better decision; taking care of Soldiers; mitigating risks; etc. Yet, MDMP does something else. MDMP is one of many processes in various professions designed to defeat **the enemy-within.**

- Are you biased?

- Is your boss biased?

- Is anyone in your unit stuck in a way of looking at things and refuses to see it from another perspective?

You get the point. Since you are human and surrounded by humans the answer to these questions is always "yes." After all, the best idea is usually yours, right? This is the enemy-within; basic bias, limited experiences, and barriers to critical thought. Without being too optimistic, the best comparison for MDMP is the Scientific Method. The reason scientists utilize the various processes of the scientific method is to overcome bias and other barriers to critical thought.

Einstein had better reasons than most of us to love his own ideas. He certainly had all the credibility anyone could ask for. He even had experience and vast knowledge. But even he was often wrong and needed processes to keep him on track. Einstein, like the rest of us, struggled to produce great ideas against time, chance, stress, and personal biases. Sound familiar?

Scientists leverage the scientific method to overcome obstacles and invite discovery. MDMP is the Army's lever to produce orders and victory on the battlefield. Since MDMP is a collaborative process involving specific processes, milestones, products, and oversight, it can be a powerful means of defeating the enemy-within. Of course, one key to defeating any enemy is understanding who the enemy is and what tactics he usually employs. The enemy-within requires the same treatment.

Here is a partial list of tactics the enemy-within will employ to keep you from making good decisions and creating effective plans:

1. Getting stuck on the person who is telling you something instead of what the person is saying. i.e. focusing on rank, personal history, personal relationship, historical credibility, etc.

    You have all kinds of people in your organization. Yes, rank matters but even a Private can have a brilliant insight, and even the commander can be wrong. There are also "crack-pots" that tend to get ignored, but maybe the strange way they see the world is just what you need to hear. Relationships are important but can lead to trusting the wrong person too much or dismissing another person too soon.

2. Association vs. Causation: "The stock market crashed on my birthday, so don't buy stocks till after my next birthday." It is tough to beat associative thinking. Few things bring out our biases quite like glazing over actual, logical cause and effect. Politicians are notorious for exploiting this aspect of human nature. All too often a leader benefits from ideas implemented by a predecessor. When the good stuff happens, the person in charge today takes credit. We associate the good thing with the current leader and move on. When looking at mission based problems it is easy to misread enemy actions and even easier to make very bad predictions based on associative bias. Basically, if you want evidence that proves your point, you can always find it.

3. The False Dilemma: "If you're not for us, you're against us." This is basically the tendency to turn complex situations into simple "A" or "B" possibilities. When a group falls into this track it will ultimately miss several other options and possible outcomes. If there is a particularly creative individual in the group, they can usually provide remedies if given the empowerment to do so. Other than that, simply forcing everyone to step away for a while (or perhaps getting the boss to step away) can work wonders.

4. Guilt by Association: "The worst commander I ever worked for wanted to do things like this, so this must be a rotten idea."

Yes, this is another flavor of associative thinking. The lure of association is very powerful. What makes this type of association different is the fact that an idea is discounted (or over credited) based on an emotional connection to a previous event, or personality, which was similar. Most units are notorious for opening old files to solve new problems. It is good to avoid re-inventing the wheel, but it is bad to think a bicycle wheel will suffice on a motorcycle. Consider this, if a dog sees an orange cone as he is struck by a vehicle, then, if he survives, he will fear orange cones and not vehicles for the rest of his life.

5. Loaded Questions: "So, why do you think this will fail?" As opposed to, "Do you think this will fail?"

Anyone who watches a tense interview on the news or a suspenseful courtroom scene observes loaded questions in action. Too often, either we, or those around us, try to shape the outcome of a discussion simply by shaping questions with a certain bend. It is often unintentional, and individuals with strong personalities and/or strong qualifications do this without thinking about it. If you hear these sorts of questions being asked and notice that the view of the situation is getting narrower and narrower, then it is time to say something.

The study of logical fallacies is a useful activity for all leaders. There are literally dozens of superb online resources to facilitate such discussions. Believe it or not, MDMP, if conducted properly, will minimize or eliminate the impact of these logical fallacies and far more. Ultimately, the goal is the development of teams that think critically and communicate effectively. Far easier said than done. However, understanding the enemy within will help.

RESPECT THE PROCESS PART 2: DEFEATING MURPHY

Ok, no one can actually beat Murphy. He always gets a vote. But, you can minimize the terrain he dominates.

Military planners have long wrangled with the fact that time and chance are rarely favorable when they are needed most. Though, it is amazing how some commanders are forever known for their ability to transform a bad turn into an axis of advance. Of course, Murphy is merely a modern metaphor. The classical understanding of the issue is usually categorized as "fog of war" or "friction." Carl Von Clausewitz is generally given credit for setting these ideas at the table of every Western military planner since 1832. Clausewitz's enduring influence is primarily rooted in the way his writing resonates Soldierly experience. As an example, read the following quote extracted from Clausewitz's seminal work, On War.

Friction is the only concept that more or less corresponds to the factors that distinguish real war from war on paper.

When you read that you know that this guy "gets it."

Everything looks much different from behind a desk with a terrain map on top of it than from an actual foxhole. When Soldiers occupy the battle position that looked so good on imagery, they discover that it is the worst place to establish security in real life. Then what do they do? How do the options affect the overall mission? Will follow-on forces and supplies be able to link-up at the new location?

Friction...Friction...Fog of War.

The Military Decision Making Process provides opportunities for commanders and their staffs to contemplate points of friction and prepare alternatives at various points. Chapter 7, which covers War-Gaming, is particularly useful in this regard.

Few things drive fear into the heart of an enemy quite like a force which can achieve the impossible or turn a disadvantage into a strong advantage. For example: Encountering a powerful river between you and the enemy and then rapidly turning a nearby forest into a bridge fit for a legion. (Julius Caesar actually did this).

RESPECT THE PROCESS PART 3: A THINKING, DETERMINED ENEMY

Another logical fallacy is the tendency to think that anyone who disagrees with you is basically an idiot. It is amazing what you do not see and do not understand when you simply write-off the knowledge and intellect of other people for any reason. The same thing happens when we assume that an inferior military force is also mentally inferior. Even worse, when we assume our adversaries view tactics and battle drills in the same manner we do. The Civil War was the last time U.S. military leaders had such a luxury. West Point graduates populated the officer ranks of both the Union and the Confederacy.

From the Battle of the Bulge to various engagements with terrorist elements during Operation Enduring Freedom (OEF) and Operation Iraqi Freedom (OIF), the enemy often reminded us that he is not stupid. This is an area that must be examined closely. Few errors are as costly in terms of real lives lost than underestimating or oversimplifying an enemy. Some refer to this tendency as "glossing over potential enemy actions" or "magic thinking."

The Army is currently developing a robust "Red Team" concept. Simply put, a staff element can, or perhaps should, have a dedicated team whose only job is determining how to best, and most efficiently, hurt the home team. You know that a staff group is doing this well when you hear a discussion like this.

S3: "We believe that enemy will rely on their base of supply here (points to map) in order to launch attacks along our flank."

Red Team Rep: "Why? I know full well you have me out-gunned. That would only expose my assets. I think it's better to disappear completely. Let you drive forward another

50 Kilometers, and then start harassing the patrol base to the south."

This notional scenario is aimed at our tendency to seek decisive engagements with enemies in the manner of Operation Anaconda, as well as our tendency to assume the enemy seeks the same thing. Perhaps they do. But don't assume so just because it would be convenient and help the long-range strategy. In the scenario above, the discussion might result in a fires plan that decimates the potential enemy course of action.

No matter how you do it, you must utilize the steps of MDMP to cultivate a thinking enemy who is determined to destroy you and everything you want to do. The *process* provides the tools. The key is to ensure you do not start thinking "magically."

MDMP IS SUPPOSED TO BE HARD... JUST LIKE A TRAFFIC CIRCLE

Even if your last MDMP experience felt like chaos, you may have still been doing it right. Which is hard to grasp because we know that when we are good at something, even if it is difficult, it feels rewarding and easy in its own way. MDMP never feels like that; even when the individuals involved are skilled, knowledgeable and experienced. The stickiness of the steps, as well as the multiple personalities that must be involved, guarantee it will always be hard.

Traffic circles are a good analogy. Although traffic circles are common in Europe, they are slowly becoming common on American roadways. American drivers do not like them. European drivers do not like them. NO one likes them...except public officials. The reason why traffic circles please public officials is the same reason why drivers don't like them. They create a moment of stress and subsequently cause drivers to exit "auto-pilot" and engage all five senses and critical thinking. In this regard, the traffic circle is like a four-way stop in a busy part of town. Even though drivers feel less safe when approaching a traffic circle (heightened senses), the result is that fewer accidents happen in and around traffic circles. This is a by-product of drivers engaged in alert, deliberate actions.

A good unit does routine things routinely. MDMP is an excellent part of that routine. However, MDMP itself should never *feel* routine.

MAKING TIME WORK FOR YOU

If you wait until the last minute, it only takes a minute.

We never have time to do it right the first time but always have time to do it over and fix it.

These are two time related clichés that haunt almost all military operations. Time is always in short supply and the more complex the task, or the more moving parts that need to get in motion, the shorter the supply of time. Here is another great one-liner that usually gets a laugh at training meetings, 'the one-third, two-thirds rule'… yeah, right. Then you are told that you need to "get your planning process ahead of headquarters' planning process." Which would put you ahead of the time crunch while simultaneously lagging behind it. The mastery of time only exists in science fiction, and yet anything close to it is a powerful weapon. In a way, time is almost a part of the enemy within.

When it comes to MDMP, time is the crucial element. You will need to know, or at least determine, the total amount of time your staff can spend on MDMP for any given order or operation. This will be the key ingredient that drives every phase and perhaps determines any modification to the process. A commander, in conjunction the XO and S3, can direct an abbreviated form of MDMP in accordance with the situation. MDMP is not necessarily a process in which less equals more (a better result), but experience and knowledge are necessary to maximize time.

Ultimately, it will be up to the Commander and the XO to determine time available for the process. Creating a good timeline for products and briefings is far more art than science. Which is why you will rarely see recommended timelines for each phase of MDMP. The number of variables involved range from the five W's of the mission, the experience and skill sets of the staff, the number of resources involved, the familiarity with the operating environment, current understanding of the enemy, etc. As you look through the detailed aspects of each phase of MDMP keep time in mind.

"KEEPING CALM" SUMMARY

- The Military Decision Making Process provides you the opportunity to take care of Soldiers and empower victory on the battlefield.

- Your greatest obstacles might be your own biases, experience, and education. What you don't know is always more plentiful than what you do, and previous results may not be the best predictors of future outcomes.

- Embrace the inherent difficulties of MDMP. It is supposed to be arduous, just like most things that produce real rewards.

- Respect time. Determine how to best break apart the time available and maximize preparation time at the Company level. *(ATTP 5-0.1 PG 4-16)*

PREPARING TO LEAD

The Power of Running in the Right Direction
(Army Design Methodology)

KEY TERMS FOR THIS CHAPTER

Army Design Methodology (ADM)—A methodology for applying critical and creative thinking to understand, visualize, and describe unfamiliar problems and approaches to solving them (ADP 5-0)

Conceptual Planning—Corresponds to the art of command and involves understanding the problem and the operational environment (ATP 5-0.1)

Detailed Planning—Translates the commander's operational approach into a complete and practical plan (ATP 5-0.1)

Commander's Visualization—The mental process of developing situational understanding, determining a desired end state, and envisioning an operational approach by which the force will achieve that end state (ADP 5-0)

Center of Gravity—the source of power that provides moral or physical strength, freedom of action, or will to act (JP 5-0)

Decisive Points—A geographic place, specific key event, critical factor, or function that, when acted upon, allows commanders to gain a marked advantage over an adversary or contribute materially to achieving success (JP 5-0)

Defeat Mechanism—The method through which friendly forces accomplish their mission against enemy opposition (ADRP 3-0)

Stability Mechanisms—The primary method where friendly forces affect civilians in order to attain conditions that support establishing a lasting, stable peace (ADRP 3-0)

Lines of Effort—A line that links multiple tasks using the logic of purpose rather than geographical reference to focus efforts toward establishing operational and strategic conditions (ADRP 3-0)

Lines of Operation—A line that defines the directional orientation of a force in time and space in relation to the enemy and that links the force with its base of operations and objectives (ADRP 3-0)

References

Army Doctrine Publication (ADP) 5-0; Dated 17 May 2012

Army Doctrine Reference Publication (ADRP) 5-0; Dated 17 May 2012

Joint Publication (JP) 5-0; Dated 11 August 2011

ATP 5-0.1; Dated 1 July 2015

If I had one hour to save the world, I would spend 55 minutes formulating the right question, and five minutes formulating the answer—Albert Einstein (maybe)

The quote above, which is often attributed to Albert Einstein (though not confirmed), is worthy of contemplation. Even if Albert Einstein did not say these words, his methods often involved looking at mysteries from a different angle. The best plans might have more to do with contemplating the actual problem than a brilliant solution.

It is difficult to avoid the temptation of getting right under the hood and turning wrenches. Moving too quickly into MDMP can be very costly without some initial reflection on the task at hand. Here is an example that you may have experienced.

A Soldier drives home and the check-engine light comes on. The Soldier is handy with basic mechanics and immediately gets under the hood. After tinkering around with a few things, it looks like a simple fix but a trip to the auto parts store is in order. To make a long story short, the Soldier spends some money and time, but ultimately finds out that the check-engine indicator was triggered by a loose gas cap. The Soldier was fully aware of this common problem, but the desire to turn wrenches in the garage and show-off mechanical skills took precedence over basic trouble shooting.

Anyone who is good at what they do and takes pride in their work can fall into the same trap. The army command and staff version of this story might resemble a commander who spins the staff up for MDMP and later realizes that a reclama1 was not only appropriate but would likely be approved.

The Army recognizes the power of answering the right question and therefore created **Army Design Methodology (ADM)** as a recommended first-stop on the way to MDMP. The most brilliant problem solving methods and teams cannot help anyone if they spin their wheels solving the wrong problem. That being said, providing subordinate units with Warning Orders (WARNOs) and the subsequent products of MDMP is essential to successful mission execution (that old one-third/two-thirds rule again). For this reason, it is important to analyze the time available to determine if ADM should take place before, simultaneously, or even after the completion of MDMP. Note, since these are all viable options, ADM should definitely have some role in the process.

Army Training Publication (ATP) 5-0.1 Army Design Methodology is the Army's source document for any and all questions pertaining to ADM.

---

1. Reclama—A request made to the authority to reconsider its decision or action. The reclama is normally sent through official channels; i.e. Through the chain of command

Army design methodology is a methodology for applying critical and creative thinking to understand, visualize, and describe unfamiliar problems and approaches to solving them (ADP 5-0). ADM includes interconnected thinking activities that aid in conceptual planning and decision making. By first framing an operational environment and associated problems, ADM enables commanders and staffs to think about the situation in depth. From this understanding, commanders and staffs develop a more informed approach to solve or manage identified problems. During operations, ADM supports organizational learning through reframing—a maturing of understanding that leads to a new perspective on problems or their resolution.

—ATP 5-0.1, dtd 1 JUL 15

As usual, the way in which fundamental concepts must be constructed in doctrine does not always make things intuitive. However, for now there are some key words to consider:

- Critical and creative thinking
- Understand
- Visualize
- Describe
- Interconnected thinking
- Conceptual planning
- Organizational learning
- New Perspective

This list is compelling evidence that ADM has the potential to bring out the best intellectual, educational, creative, and experiential qualities from staff officers and NCOs. It is a semi-formal, loosely structured way to embrace the reality of just how complex many of the problems we face really are.

For this type of process, we are talking about **Conceptual Planning** as opposed to **Detailed Planning**. In order to win, you need both. ADM provides the framework for conceptual planning and MDMP provides the structure for detailed planning. Yet, have you ever noticed how new information can change everything? When you get into the nuts and bolts of MDMP new information and insights happen every minute. This means, naturally, that the conceptual understanding needs to change as well. Therefore, ADM is always on-going to some degree.

The following chart is pulled from ATP 5-0.1 and illustrates the ADM/MDMP continuum.

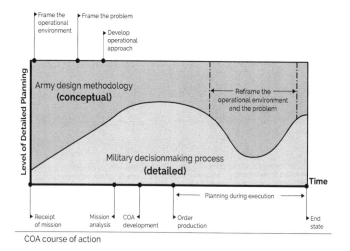

The bottom of the chart places the steps of MDMP in sequence and the curve is an estimate of the intensity of detailed planning in each phase. Note, each step along both the top and bottom will be discussed throughout this book.

Look at the upper right portion of the chart. It says, "Reframe the operational environment and the problem." Then notice that this is hovering above the block of time that occurs AFTER Order Production.

Wait a minute.

Once we kick out an order we've crossed the finish line and moved on to bigger and better things. Right? That is the most natural tendency, and a good staff has plenty on their plates at any given time. But until an End State is reached our attitude must shift from 'putting things in the rear-view mirror,' to 'seeing things through to the end.' Operational and tactical units will do amazing things with METT-TC[32] as they adapt and maneuver through the mission, but those changes also change the entire concept. A good commander and staff owe their expertise and planning skills to those units all the way to the objective.

---

2. METT-TC—Mission, Enemy, Terrain and Weather, Troops and Support Available, Time Available, and Civil Considerations

ADM AND MDMP, LIKE EVERYTHING ELSE, ARE COMMAND DRIVEN

The primary thing to keep in mind during ADM, as with everything else, is the commander. Army Design Methodology is, in effect, a deliberate method for commanders and staff elements to develop what army doctrine calls *the commander's visualization.* The fact that the word "visualization" is the primary goal should tell you that ADM is striving for conceptual outcomes. Try to resist nailing down detailed nuts and bolts that are designated for MDMP. Problem solving can be invigorating and take on a life of its own, but the key is to properly represent the way that the commander envisions the problem.

The commander's visualization consists of three components as illustrated in ADRP 5-0 and JP 5-0.

Current Situation	Operational Approach	End State
Described by current conditions		Described by desired future conditions
Army design methodology and mission analysis help the commander and staff develop understanding.	From their understanding of the current situation, mission, and desired end state, commanders conceptualize an operational approach to attain the end state.	Commanders visualize the operation's end state in term of desired future conditions.

If you can fill in these blocks with some certainty and have data/analysis to back it up, then ADM is more or less complete, but more is better. This chapter will provide food for thought regarding the prioritization of design methods in your planning processes.

GETTING READY FOR ADM

During any training event, unit activity, or ceremony, it is important to have the right people, in the right frame of mind, with the right equipment, at the right place, and the right time. ADM is no different.

The Right People

➢ Expertise from across the staff sections as well as input from the commander

➢ Think about the right number of participants (too many is worse than too few)

➢ Consider rank, experience, and professional education

➢ Consider personal dynamics and conflicts that may arise (temperament)

➢ Who are the visual thinkers?

➢ Who are the logical ones?

➢ Who has a good understanding of enemy TTPs?

➢ Who do the others respect or tend to listen to?

➢ Who will the leader actually be?

➢ Who often acts like 'a thorn in the flesh?' (you need this person)

➢ Who is a peacemaker?

➢ Who is a good recorder?

➢ Who is a good negotiator?

➤ And then,

➤ Who will you swap out half-way through to break up the Group Think that will most likely emerge?

❖ (Groups tend to start out with multiple perspectives and eventually adopt mutual blinders. A fresh set of eyes mitigates this.)

THE RIGHT FRAME OF MIND

ADM is about creativity, problem solving, and exchanging ideas. The right tone and environment are essential. The team should be given some rules of engagement and expectations.

· Widest participation is the goal

· All opinions (except deliberate disruption) are valuable

· Make a practice of repeating back new concepts and ideas i.e. "Your saying that this road might be more of a factor than we believe. Is that right?"

· Remain curious and open minded

· Accept that things are and may remain ambiguous (do not rush to simplify or "fix" the problem)

· Accept that your ideas will be critiqued and pulled apart

· Consider which things can be confirmed and which will stay an assumption

· Consider removing ranks, mentally for sure, literally as a possibility

- Set realistic goals

- Set break times in which members disengage and allow thoughts and solutions to settle in. We've all had those a-ha moments where long sought solutions suddenly pop into our heads as we are sitting down to lunch.

- Side-bars are good but respect for the process is pre-eminent

- Watch out for the group leaning too much on one or two individuals

- Watch out for one or two individuals taking over

THE RIGHT EQUIPMENT

- Notebooks

- Pens, Pencils, Markers

- Whiteboard(s)

- Butcher block paper

- Pins or tape (for putting sketches or other graphics and notes on the walls

- A computer, projector and screen

- Sufficient room space and table space

- Beverages and snacks

- Sticky-note pads

The Right Place

Aside from a space large enough to comfortably facilitate such an activity it is also important to think about the impact on physical arrangements of space. Problem solving and group dynamics are easily impacted by elbow room, heat/cold, lighting, ambient noise, etc. In terms of an arrangement that encourages collaboration, consider this figure from ATP 5-0.1.

Discouraging dialogue

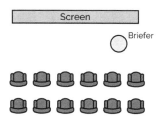

Encouraging dialogue

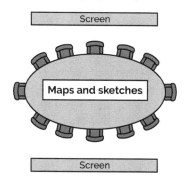

FRAMING THE QUESTION—PROBLEM STATEMENT

During the initial phase of ADM the team will need to remember that **the goal is to discover the right question, not a best solution.** Solutions will take shape in the latter half of ADM. Now that the conditions are set for the conduct of ADM it is time to get into nuts and bolts of the process. Note, because this is ADM and therefore conceptual in nature, this is not a Step 1, Step 2, Step 3 system with distinct inputs and outputs at each phase. You will get plenty of that when we get into MDMP.

Few things get after the "5th W" or "Why" quite like ADM. *It is one thing to have an amazing plan with massing effects and a dynamic scheme of maneuver that 'takes the hill' to reach a decisive point in a mission, but is quite another to know that hill was worth taking in the first place.*

The overall goal of ADM is very simple; just follow these three points (which closely resemble the CDR's visualization).

❖ You are at a point in time with certain conditions and resources

❖ You want to get to another point in time with certain conditions and resources.

❖ <u>How do you connect those points in time (and space), or what is the main obstacle that must be overcome?</u>

Hence, ADM gets after the key question(s) connecting these points in time. It is really a very simple proposal, however, the space between the first two points is usually a darkened maze filled with cobwebs, blind corners, moving walls, two-way mirrors, and the occasional tiger-trap. ADM is ambiguous throughout the process and you will not get it right the first time.

Looking at the first two bullets (start point and end point conditions), it becomes clear that someone needs to decide what information really matters. In the age of Google, information about almost anything is infinite. The commander plays a vital role in helping to determine the most relevant and critical conditions the staff should focus on. For instance, the start point might be in the presence of a terrorist cell within the unit's area of operations. Imagine all the people, places, and things that are involved in analyzing that group's activities. Without some initial guidance to guide the analysis there will never be enough time to get the job done.

Here is one graphic from ATP 5-0.1 that illustrates this concept and problem solving approach. It is a comparison of the current state and the future state.

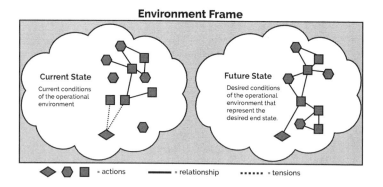

The primary elements of this analysis are actors, relationships, and tensions. The analysis will probably determine how things got to this point, where it is likely to go if nothing is done, what are the greatest threats, and what works in our favor. If you have spent time with MDMP and other staff processes you might recognize this sort of graphic as a Center of Gravity (CoG) approach. There will be plenty more on COG later.

Caution: *Models are very powerful tools that organize thoughts and communicate complicated things. However, they also shape the discussion and the way that people think about facts. If you consider, from a couple paragraphs back, the way in which you considered analyzing a terrorist threat, it might be different then how you see it now. Chances are, that as soon as you saw "actors, relationships, and tensions," you immediately began to hang your thoughts on that tree. It might be valuable to allow the group to work without a model for a short time and simply analyze initial conditions as they are. However, before ADM starts, research a few different models that might work for this mission. Once the ideas, discussions, and notes start taking shape the commander or designated representative could suggest a model or two that might work best based on where things are going. At some point, a model is going to be far more helpful than distracting.*

Army Design Methodology gets the mental juices flowing and people tend to go off on tangents or "rabbit trails" during discussions. Without some fixed guideposts, a battalion level

ADM session could turn into a strategic policy workgroup in short order. Keep the following "range fans" in mind (and perhaps put them on the wall at the start of ADM):

- Higher headquarters guidance and direction
- Focus on the things your unit can affect with its resources
- Recognize things that will not change (i.e. cultural identity of target population)
- Recognize things that, even if they did change, would not help you reach the objective.

Note: *"Rabbit trails" should be allowed for a short time. The result will often be notes that turn into requests for information (RFIs) and request for resources and enablers. After all, arresting a certain individual fifty miles away might not be within your unit's authority or resources, but once higher headquarters knows why you want it done they might agree and task it out.*

The commander, or command representative, should keep tabs with the ADM process and realize when an understanding of the current state and the desired future state is culminating. At that time, develop a product that summarizes the groups conclusions. During MDMP this product is referred to as Problem Statement (See Chapter 5: MDMP Step Two). This is one way in which ADM directly feeds MDMP and the orders process. A Problem Statement is usually expressed as a narrative. A narrative is something that, even at the platoon level, most leaders are familiar with. It usually reads something like this:

> *The population of Centerville is approximately 5000 people but they exert great influence in our Operational Environment (OE). There are three prominent families with ancient connections to the area who hold most governing roles and control much of the local economy. In the last two years, extra-judicial killings began targeting members of the Alpha family and as a result the Bravo and Charlie families were suspected and sometimes blamed. Based on intelligence estimates there is reason to believe that this violence is the work of local terrorist networks who want to destabilize historical stability and insert their influence with the local population. Centerville is an important part of the center region's economy and security and needs stabilization.*

The narrative should be supported by concise notes, graphics, maps, models, etc. and then be briefed to the commander. The commander will most likely consider the key elements that higher headquarters are looking for as well as any new information. Additionally, he or she will look for areas where too many assumptions were made, or perhaps evidence that the team determined a solution early on and shaped the statement to that end. In the above narrative, it would be a dead give-away if the last sentence was, "arresting or killing (fill in name) will put an end to the violence."

While it may be the case that eliminating a certain individual would solve the problem, the current phase is supposed to be about discovering the correct problem, not finding the solution.

DETERMINING AN OPERATIONAL APPROACH

Determining an operational approach is when the solution to the problem begins to take shape. An operational approach is the commander's visualization of what needs to be done to solve or manage identified problems (ATP 5-0.1). After evaluating where we are and defining where we want to go it is time to consider the obstacles and, more specifically, *main obstacle* in our way. The obstacle could be a person, an enemy maneuver element, a hostile population, or a literal obstacle (mine field, river, damaged road, etc.). There is likely to be more than one means of removing or by-passing each type of obstacle. Once the commander and staff determine what must be overcome and the most effective way to do so, they will have an operational approach.

If that does not sound like a military course of action (COA), then that is good. They are supposed to be different. Think of an operational approach as, 'remove the mayor of Centerville from power.' In this case, a COA would look like, 'support fair elections by providing security.' More violent or direct variations of removing the current mayor would constitute other COAs.

The following graphic from ATP 5-0.1 demonstrates how the environmental frame from the first half of ADM is expanded to include the elements of determining an operational approach.

Environment Frame

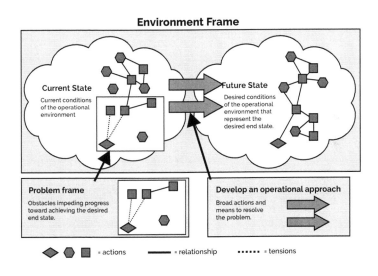

DETERMINE FRIENDLY AND ENEMY CENTERS OF GRAVITY

A **center of gravity** is the source of power that provides moral or physical strength, freedom of action, or will to act (JP 5-0).

In general, the analysis, determination, and expression of the center of gravity is a big deal in U.S. military doctrine and has been for generations. The definition from JP 5-0 is more or less lifted word for word from Carl Von Clausewitz's On War (depending on the translation of course). Clausewitz is generally given credit for solidifying the concept of center of gravity and permanently fixing it into western military strategy and tactics. Behind the scenes , however, modern scholars and theorists debate the merits of the concept and try to determine whether technology, cyber, irregular warfare, and cultural realities have made the concept irrelevant. In reality, such considerations do make for excellent professional development opportunities and facilitate in depth discussion about our complex world and military planning. Another reality is the fact that, until some global shift in doctrine occurs, you need to accept and understand the concept of CoG.

Think of a historical battle or conflict that you are familiar with. When you consider the elements that create an effective army it is a complex picture:

- Size of the Army

- Technology and weapon systems

- The will of the people to support the effort

- The talent and charisma of the national leader

- The tactical talents of the military leadership

- Logistical hubs

- Terrain, roads, rivers, etc.

These are only a few pieces of a complex puzzle. The question is, which piece is THE piece i.e. the Center of Gravity? Perhaps a single, massive defeat of a large field army will break the enemy. Perhaps the elimination of one key general will do it. Maybe the destruction of one port, one factory, or one rail system will do. Maybe the people are near rebellion and leaning on them will do the trick. The possibilities are endless and yet CoG analysis requires that some method must determine, not a combination of things that our efforts must work on, but THE thing.

A classic example is the fact that many leaders within the Allied forces in WWII did not believe that eliminating Hitler would be as viable a CoG as much as the elimination of one or two of his generals. This view leads to the discussion that Hitler then attacked his own CoG when he presented Field Marshall Rommel with little choice but to commit suicide.

It may sound like an impossible if not pointless pursuit, but the better you understand a system the less ridiculous it becomes. Turn the lens around and ask yourself what you believe is the most vulnerable aspect of your unit. Haven't you heard people say something to the effect of, "If they lost that 1SG over there, the whole unit would just collapse." Of course, such statements require a grain of salt, but there is usually more than a grain of truth to it. The point is that the best method for determining a center of gravity is a dedicated, disciplined study of yourself and the enemy.

Like everything else, CoG analysis will require a model so that the commander and staff can visualize and evaluate the validity of a CoG. The chart below might look like something you've seen before. It is only one way that CoG can be visualized.

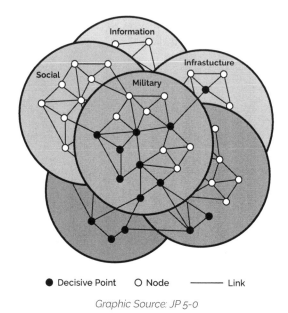

● Decisive Point   O Node   ——— Link

Graphic Source: JP 5-0

The above graphic relies on an analysis of the operational variables PMESII (political, military, economic, social, infrastructure, and information systems), but perhaps a situation would call for METT-TC, or ASCOPE (Area Structures Capabilities Organizations People and Events), or something else. The commander, in conjunction with senior staff members, will most likely direct the method for CoG analysis. Perhaps one way to consider the value and a method of CoG analysis is to consider that a military operation is the application of a large amount of military force while firing a rifle is a small amount. Just as a marksman needs a small bullseye to maximize the application of skill, discipline, and lethality, then so does the organization. Joint Publication 5-0 provides several models, methods, and details regarding Center of Gravity analysis.

Variable	Description
Mission	Commanders and staffs view all of the mission variables in terms of their impact on mission accomplishment. The mission is the task, together with the purpose, that clearly indicates the action to be taken and the reason therefore. It is always the first variable commanders consider during decisionmaking. A mission statement contains the "who, what, when, where, and why" of the operation.
Enemy	The second variable to consider is the enemy—dispositions (including organization, strength, location, and tactical mobility), doctrine, equipment, capabilities, vulnerabilities, and probable courses of action.
Terrain and weather	Terrain and weather analysis are inseparable and directly influence each other's impact on military operations. Terrain includes natural features (such as rivers and mountains) and man-made features (such as cities, airfields, and bridges). Commanders analyze terrain using the five military aspects of terrain expressed in the memory aid OAKOC: observation and fields of fire, avenues of approach, key and decisive terrain, obstacles, cover and concealment. The military aspects of weather include visibility, wind, precipitation, cloud cover, temperature, and humidity.

Troops and support available	This variable includes the number, type, capabilities, and condition of available friendly troops and support. These include supplies, services, and support available from joint, host nation, and unified action partners. They also include support from civilians and contractors employed by military organizations, such as the Defense Logistics Agency and the Army Materiel Command.
Time available	Commanders assess the time available for planning, preparing, and executing tasks and operations. This includes the time required to assemble, deploy, and maneuver units in relationship to the enemy and conditions.
Civil considerations	Civil considerations are the influence of man-made infrastructure, civilian institutions, and activities of the civilian leaders, populations, and organizations within an area of operations on the conduct of military operations (ADRP 5-0). Civil considerations comprise six characteristics, expressed in the memory aid ASCOPE: areas, structures, capabilities, organizations, people, and events.

Source for chart: FM 6-0

PMESII-PT

- **Political.** This variable describes the distribution of responsibility and power at all levels of governance—formally constituted authorities, as well as informal or covert political powers. (Who is the tribal leader in the village?)

- **Military.** This variable includes the military and paramilitary capabilities of all relevant actors (enemy, friendly, and neutral) in a given operational environment. (Does the enemy in this particular neighborhood have antitank systems?)

- **Economic.** This variable encompasses individual and group behaviors related to producing, distributing, and consuming resources. (Does the village have a high unemployment rate?)

- **Social.** This variable includes the cultural, religious, and ethnic makeup within an operational environment and the beliefs, values, customs, and behaviors of society members. (Who are the influential people in the village—for example, religious leaders, tribal leaders, warlords, criminal bosses, or prominent families?)

- **Information.** This variable describes the nature, scope, characteristics, and effects of individuals, organizations, and systems that collect, process, disseminate, or act on information. (How much access does the local population have to news media or the Internet?)

- Infrastructure. This variable comprises the basic facilities, services, and installations needed for the functioning of a community or society. (Is the electrical generator in the village working?)

- **Physical Environment.** This variable includes the geography and man-made structures, as well as the climate and weather in the area of operations. (What types of terrain or weather conditions in this area of operations favor enemy operations?)

- **Time.** This variable describes the timing and duration of activities, events, or conditions within an operational environment, as well as how the timing and duration are perceived by various actors in the operational environment. (For example, at what times are people likely to congest roads or conduct activities that provide a cover for hostile operations?)

DECISIVE POINTS

Decisive points which are not to be confused with decision points. While there may be several things about the mission that could be a decisive point, the goal should be to determine THE decisive point. *A decisive point is a geographic place, specific key event, critical factor, or function that, when acted upon, allows commanders to gain a marked advantage over an adversary or contribute materially to achieving success (JP 5-0).*

The decisive point may be securing a bridge, or a road. The capture or elimination of an enemy leader could also be a decisive point. Ultimately, once friendly forces reach the decisive point, if it was analyzed correctly, the momentum and initiative should be heavily in favor of friendly forces from that point forward. Simply put, the decisive point puts your unit at "first and goal."

DEFEAT MECHANISMS AND STABILITY MECHANISMS

A ***defeat mechanism*** *is the method through which friendly forces accomplish their mission against enemy opposition (ADRP 3-0). Defeat mechanisms are generally associated with combat* *operations and bring physical or psychological defeat upon the enemy. There are four doctrinal defeat mechanisms that can and should be used simultaneously or in complementary combination (Definitions from ATP 5-0.1).*

- **Destroy**—Apply lethal combat power on an enemy capability so that it no longer performs any function and cannot be restored to a usable condition without rebuilding

- **Dislocate**—Employ forces to obtain significant positional advantage, rendering the enemy's disposition less valuable, perhaps even irrelevant.

- **Disintegrate**—Disrupt the enemy's command and control system, degrading the ability to conduct operations while leading to a rapid collapse of the enemy's capabilities or will to fight

- **Isolate**—deny an enemy or adversary access to capabilities that enable the exercise of coercion, influence, potential advantage, and freedom of action.

*A **stability mechanism** is the primary method where friendly forces affect civilians in order to attain conditions that support establishing a lasting, stable peace* (ADRP 3-0). Stability mechanisms are usually attached to stability actions. Whereas defeat mechanisms usually focus on enemy military forces, stability mechanisms target a particular population. The population itself may be the COG. In such a case, it would be no surprise that both the enemy and friendly forces share the same COG (Definitions from ATP 5-0.1).

- **Compel**—Use, or threaten to use, lethal force to establish control and dominance, affect behavioral change, or enforce compliance with mandates, agreements, or civil authority

- **Control**—(Within the context of stability) imposing civil order via securing borders, routes, sensitive sites, population centers, and individuals. It also involves physically occupying key terrain and facilities.

- **Influence**—To alter the opinions and attitudes of a civilian population or change behaviors through nonlethal means

- **Support**—Establishing, reinforcing, or setting the conditions necessary for other instruments of national power to function effectively

LINES OF EFFORT AND LINES OF OPERATIONS

The first part of this chapter dealt with determining exactly where/how things are in the present and then determining how they should be in the future. Connecting those two points in time is the trick. Once the ADM process produces a detailed analysis of current and desired conditions it is time to literally connect the dots. Lines of effort (LOE) and lines of operations (LOO) are those connections. The biggest difference between the two lines is LOOs track pertains to maneuver while LOEs pertain to civil security or assistance to local governance, in essence, combat operations vs. stability *efforts*. On the next page is a sample diagram of an LOO and LOE from ATP 5-0.1.

There are usually several LOOs and/or LOEs pertaining to an operation. This method can provide clarity and focus especially when the lines are connected to objectives and those objectives press toward the center of gravity.

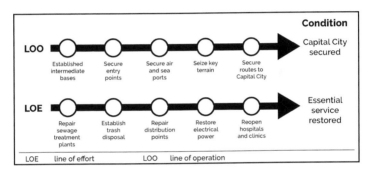

CONSOLIDATE AND PREPARE FOR MDMP

Army Design Methodology may not always be a formal or deliberate part of the orders process but it does happen. At some point in time someone decides exactly what the unit needs to do and how it should do it. The objectives of ADM are essential to any coherent order. Therefore, a deliberate approach to defining these essential elements of the planning process is worthy of consideration.

Whether you used ADM, another design method, or just some quick notes in your green book from the boss, you should have the following things lined up as you begin MDMP.

- ✓ An understanding of current conditions

- ✓ An understanding of desired conditions

- ✓ An understanding of the main obstacle between current and desired conditions

- ✓ Identification of the center of gravity

- ✓ An initial assessment of decisive points

- ✓ A determination of which mechanisms (defeat/stability) you intend to employ (operational approach)

At a minimum, you should be able to fill in the three blocks of the Commander's Visualization.

1. Current Situation

2. Operational Approach

3. End State

And the most essential element: An acceptance that ADM is an enduring process—all points are subject to questioning and change until the operation is complete.

DON'T FORGET THE REGS.

Maybe you've heard something like this during a back-brief or planning session.

New S3 OIC: "Sir, we will hit the objective no later than 1700 and take the enemy out."

Battalion Commander: "Hit the objective? Open or closed fist? Take the enemy out? You mean like, for pizza?"

The words the S3 was looking for were, most likely, attack and destroy. It is best to acclimate yourself to doctrinal words until they are second nature during long and often stressful briefings to senior leaders. A good XO or Chief of Staff will most likely enforce this habit at all times. A successful career is built, in part, on recognizing bad habits and taking the time and effort to change.

At some point, it will be second nature to consult a few key regulations during planning, however, pay close attention when these regulations are updated or amended. New terms spring up overnight and these changes are often driven by the highest levels of command and new priorities. The staff, probably more than any other element, are essential to solidifying new terminology into daily operations.

Staff Officer/NCO Starter Library—

- ADRP 1-02

- ADP 5-0

- ADRP 5-0

- FM 6-0

"SOLVE THE RIGHT PROBLEM" SUMMARY

- The Army Design Methodology (ADM) is a framework that allows commanders and their staffs to explore the current condition, the desired condition, and the best method of transition to the desired condition.

- Leaders should take a deliberate approach to ADM and assign the right people with the right frame of mind for the task.

- A center of gravity (CoG) is the source of power that provides moral or physical strength, freedom of action, or will to act

- Most operations benefit from both Lines of Operation and Lines of Effort. Do not overlook one just because the nature of a mission will lean heavily on the other

- Prepare for Step One of MDMP with an understanding of what your unit is trying to do and the mechanism it should employ to do it...then keep an open mind regarding changes.

12

DON'T BE A LEMMING

SOCIAL PROOFING

Maybe it is just a sense of safety in numbers or maybe it is just laziness, but no matter where you look, people are utilizing other people as a substitute for Critical Thinking. If a million fans can't be wrong, then what about ten million, or a hundred million? There is something to be said about consensus when reputations and fortunes are clearly on the line.

Afterall, if a famous musician can have any guitar they wish and their career relies on their performance, then that says something about the one that they take on stage. Then again, there is something to be learned from lemmings. In case you do not know, lemmings have one claim to fame and that is running madly in mass numbers to a cliff where they all plunge to their deaths.

Nature is just full of contradictory lessons. There are the lemmings and then there are dolphins and even some rodents that rely on safety in numbers. Perhaps the lesson is that if you have chance to step away from the crowd and apply some Critical Thinking, then maybe you can sort the dolphins from the lemmings. There must be a better way to put that. However, if it stands out enough to stick in your memory, then that is the goal.

The world of financial scandals is full of lessons that never seem to stick. People probably know better, but when everyone else seems to be cashing in, it is hard to resist getting in while the getting is good. Interestingly, there are many winners amid massive failures but, much like lottery winners, they are the tiny minority. If you spend much time around a casino, you learn that way too many big winners holding large award checks in framed photos along the gaming halls stayed at the casino that same night long enough to lose it all again.

It takes practice to develop the emotional skill of putting passions aside long enough to think through any situation.

Let's take a look at some famous scandals and discover why social proofing took over and why Critical Thinking helped some people win the day.

CHARLES PONZI

You have probably heard of the Ponzi Scheme even if you do not understand it or know anyone who has lost money to one. The Ponzi Scheme was usually known as the "rob Peter to pay Paul" scheme prior to the spectacular events of 1920 that made Charles Ponzi a legend in the annuls of financial scandal. The Watergate Scandal created a new paradigm where the media can't help but report political scandals in terms of a "-gate" nomenclature, i.e. Travelgate, Spygate, Russiagate, Emailgate, etc. Accordingly, it seems that no financial scandal will ever be so large as to deprive Charles Ponzi of his credit for the "Ponzi Scheme."

The Ponzi Scheme is very basic. Convince a group of people that you can deliver incredible returns on investment, collect their money, use that money to return large "dividends" to the initial investors and let those investors tell their friends about the incredible deal. The number of investors will likely go ten-fold, which allows the schemer to turn the new money over into more and more dividends. Of course, most of the money is kept in the account of the schemer. Most Ponzi schemers keep a *large* amount of cash on hand for payout so that if anyone asks for their capital back, they can usually get it back. This then feeds the sense that the investment opportunity is legitimate. Afterall, people get returns and anyone with second thoughts gets their money back with no questions asked.

You see, the even though the scammer must give up some significant chunks of cash on demand, they gain social proof in return. That social proof generates new investors in waves. The short-term sacrifice of funds is well worth it.

Of course, the math always runs out on such scams because eventually you run out of new money to fund old clients. Interestingly, Charles Ponzi is far more complicated than the stereotype of capitalistic greedy boogeymen. His was a rags to riches immigrant story loaded with countless acts of charity and generosity along the way. He was known for charity long before he was known for having any money in his pocket. How many people do you know that would donate several feet of their own skin to assist a burn victim they didn't even know? Charles Ponzi did just that. This was part of the reason why people lined up at his door to invest in his scheme, but you would be hard pressed to see evidence that he made such sacrifices as part of a scammer's long game. There is every indication that his extreme charity was genuine and motivated the hardships he experienced in his own life prior to financial prominence.

These points are brought up in the hopes that they will encourage a less simplistic understanding of significant persons in history. Simplifying and stereotyping are the enemies of critical thinking. Take a closer look at any part of history that you believe you know well, and you will be surprised. Many people have something to gain by putting all events into convenient boxes, but you have much more to gain by discovering the reality for yourself.

Charles Ponzi managed to rake in the equivalent of 32 million dollars in less than one year thanks almost entirely to social proofing. There is every indication that Charles Ponzi was hit unexpectedly by the tidal wave of investors and may have simply been overtaken by his own success. Afterall, very few people have the wherewithal to say, "No thank you, I am not ready for your money. Please come back when my business model is more mature."

Anyway, here is where Critical Thinking should have taken over. Ponzi was basically offering what today would be known as a FOREX or currency trading scheme. He realized that multiple nations agreed on the price of postage for mail in the aftermath of WWI. However, some countries' currency was worth far more than others in the post-war world. Imagine if could purchase something for 1 U.S. Dollar and the sell it for 1 Kuwaiti Dinar. This would allow you to profit 3 dollars per transaction.

In Ponzi's case the only trick would be early twentieth century costs of travel that would eat up a decent portion of the profits. However, to investors, it sounded like Ponzi discovered a money printing mechanism and he did little to inform them that he did not actually have the logistics in place.

Here is the problem, and this is where some of the more astute investors and other critical thinkers avoided the scheme. You do not need to be a mathematician to realize that if the profit margin per postage certificate is roughly 25 cents on average after expenses, then it would take 4 million postage transactions to generate a million dollars in revenue. Ponzi was bringing in several million dollars in investment capital. Does that sound like something that is feasible? Was there any evidence that someone was purchasing that many pieces of postage and selling them back in different countries? Wouldn't that cause problems for the postal system and cause the postmasters to update their policies and laws? Were there enough postage certificates in circulation to facilitate this? Why was Ponzi keeping such large cash reserves in local banks? Shouldn't those assets be used to purchase more postage? How can you turn investments into profits if the investments are sitting in a bank? Why would you allow capital to sit in a bank when you have the means to double it at will?

The numbers did not add up and it was clear that Ponzi was not using investment capital for his alleged money-making venture. It should have seemed clear that Ponzi's bank accounts were filled with initial investment money and not the profits of an innovative new money-making method. However, such is nature of social proof and fear of missing opportunity that thousands ignored the warning signs and ended up losing their money.

BERNIE MADOFF

There's no need to belabor the point. Bernie Madoff is probably the most famous financial scammer in living memory. His scheme was identical to Charles Ponzi. However, Bernie

Madoff enhanced his profile in the investment community by creating a sense that you had to be invited into the scheme. In other words, there was not only the compelling factor of social proof but also a sense of being lucky because you were now going to be part of an exclusive elite.

When the world saw Bernie Madoff, they saw prominent people and celebrities that were having success with Mr. Madoff and everyone knows that celebrities can work with anyone they want. Therefore, Bernie must be legitimate and the best. After all, this guy was once chairman of the NASDAQ, he must know what he is doing, he wouldn't risk everything on a fraud. All the insiders seem to agree. How could this be wrong?

However, the same warning signs were there. Why keep such large reserves on hand if you have the magic touch in turning the largest consistent profits in the industry? How is it possible that year after year there was never a downturn, even when everyone else inevitably reported losses from time to time? How is it possible that other investment gurus who had basically the same approach to investments could not do half as well as Madoff?

The biggest trick to Critical Thinking will always be turning emotions and bias down to hear the truth in the background. Social proof and the fear of missing out on an opportunity tend to speak louder than logic.

THERANOS

Sometimes our political sensibilities and emotional connection to someone's life story cause us to overlook details and ignore otherwise obvious red flags. Theranos is another modern legend in terms of presenting the world with a multi-billion-dollar scam. The founder of Theranos, Elizabeth Holmes, was everything that most people wanted her to be. She was another promising tech genius who dropped out of an Ivy league college at age 19 to pursue a vision that would change the world. Before long, she was the youngest female self-made billionaire in history and circulating among Silicon Valley's elite. This is the sort of story that basically everyone was ready to see and glad to accept.

Her vision was relatively simple. She wanted to make providing blood samples less painful and much simpler. Imaging a device the size of a desktop computer that could run a dozen or more tests with only a couple drops of blood. There is no indication that her vision was not sincere and that she believed for one moment that it could not be done. However, in time, it did become clear that the Edison Device was simply not possible, and it appeared that she began to structure the organization so as to prevent this terrible secret from becoming obvious to everyone.

In the meantime, Elizabeth was getting personal visits from past and current Presidents, showing up on any number of magazine covers, and basically became someone other celebrities and public figures wanted to be seen with. Her board of directors included John Mattis, Henry Kissinger, former congressional leaders, and former Fortune 500 CEOs. Rubert Murdoch, Walgreens, and others were investing millions in Theranos, and before long, it looked like Edison devices were up and working in the Walgreens around the corner. It was even widely known that one of Elizabeth Holmes' former professors left his position with Stanford to work for her. What could possibly be wrong with Theranos?

In terms of Critical Thinking there were some who looked at Theranos and saw a lot of important people getting involved but none of them had backgrounds in biomedical research or innovation. Shouldn't something as critical as informing people about their health by way of blood test have prominent medical researchers on the board? It seemed like the Theranos board was more about generating a list of people with the highest levels of social proof than finding the people that ought to be there.

The other issues were a little more along the lines of common sense. We may not understand the technical reasons why a drop of blood supplying the necessary material for multiple tests would represent an exponential revolution in many fields, but we do know that if one entire vial is needed for one test, then one drop for multiple tests seems like a bit of a stretch.

Theranos is an interesting case study because there were so many factors which individually tend to sidetrack Critical Thinking, but when combined it borders on blasphemy to question Elizabeth Holmes and her vision.

Aside from the good news story of seeing the youngest self-made female tech mogul take Silicon Valley by storm, we also saw some of the most respectable and prominent people put their reputations on the line to join the organization. However, there was more at work. Why would we accept that one drop of blood could inform doctors on life-or-death issues across multiple tests? Very simply, people have romantic notions and high expectations regarding technological progress.

Anyone who was born in a world without home computers and now holds the world in the palm of their hand with a smartphone can be convinced that almost anything is around the next corner. The fact that former executives from Apple were also on board with Theranos just contributed to the idea that another giant leap on technological progress was here.

However, warning signs are warning signs and if people start acting defensive or evasive when simple questions are put forward, it is time to put your Critical Thinking in overdrive even if the results will break your heart and dampen your dreams.

ENRON

Maybe you remember the George W. Bush era Wall Street scandal that happened under the banner of Enron. They were another group of financiers that basically fooled them all until the truth could not be contained anymore. But what was Enron?

Enron began as an energy supply company that moved on to facilitating investments in Energy Futures and basically anything that could be gambled on, including the weather. Before long, they were the talk of Wall Street and became known as the company that could not lose. However, the warning signs were there even early in the company's history.

In 1997, here was an event known at the time as the Valhalla Scandal. It turns out that two traders within ENRON were committing outright fraud to produce returns. When the traders were caught, they were not fired, but instead congratulated by the senior leaders of the ENRON. The traders were told to go out and keep making the company money. Clearly, there was a corporate climate at Enron that should have concerned investors and motivated regulators to zoom in on their operations.

Another warning sign with Enron was the fact that, like Ponzi and Madoff, they just kept winning. No matter how savvy or lucky a business or investor is, they will eventually endure down times and post losses. Not only that, but Enron barely had any debt to tear down their profits. How did they do it?

Enron was not a Ponzi scheme. In fact, they were no different than most average investing firms and, their returns were below average. Their real numbers were actually very concerning, but to cover for that, Enron used an accounting trick. They decided to post projected profits as current profits. This meant that an investment that was supposed to return $10 million dollars over ten years would hit the books as a $10 million dollar profit today.

No, you can't do that. Any auditor would see this and notify both the SEC and investors about Enron's fraudulent bookkeeping. However, Enron was audited and always passed. What could people do but see the firm as a legitimate wonderchild in action. How did they pass audit?

They didn't.

Look out, here comes your trust in watch dog organizations to derail your Critical Thinking. Afterall, as long as the FBI, the SEC, a state bureau of investigation, a prominent journalist, or a top auditing firm says, "nothing to see here," then it must be so.

What if a prominent watch dog is willing to risk losing everything for a big payout under the table? No one would do that, right? Who on earth would give up decades of public trust and reputation to face ruin, embarrassment, and bankruptcy?

Well, it can all be yours if the price is right.

In January of 2001, there were *five* auditing agencies that investors looked to as referees for the investment trade. In December of 2001, Enron's tricky bookkeeping was revealed and now there are *four* auditing agencies on Wall Street. The now defunct auditors who worked for Arthur Anderson took the big gamble and lost. Up until December 2001 the auditors, the stockbrokers, Forbes magazine, and the day trader down the block were all telling you the same thing. How can you see past institutional and social proof as strong as that?

Once again, the answer is cultivating a little emotional detachment and trusting your instincts. If something seems to be too good to be true, then at the very least, there is more there than meets the eye. Start asking hard questions and see what happens.

CONCLUSION

The list of financial scandals and crashes that could and should have been avoided goes on and on. Remember the "dot com" bubble when people were willing to put $10 Million into a startup that barely had an office and two employees just because they might be the next big thing?

What about the Real Estate crash?

No matter where you look, there are always people who can see that there is something wrong and stand on their convictions while everyone else laughs. When people look back, they see that the warning signs were obvious but emotions and feeding frenzy mentality kept people from seeing the obvious. When it came to the real estate crash, there was a man named Michael Burry who was willing to stake everything on the fact that the housing market was about to collapse. Everyone thought he was crazy, but time vindicated him.

With all these examples, it should be said that real, genuine, legitimate successes will also have high levels of social proof. Millions of people flock to hear certain musicians or read books by certain authors. When there is excellence, it will attract a crowd of highly appreciative fans. The lesson of this chapter is not ignoring popular and trending successes because they may be frauds, but to use Critical Thinking to verify if the hype has been earned.

It may be counterintuitive to seek out a professional with a small number of views vs. another with millions of followers. But real, hard-working professionals are usually working hard at their business and not generating several pieces of slick-looking content every day. They will end up looking less professional on social media, but if someone on your timeline says they are a trusted expert in a profession, but they never seem to speak about details or devote most of their waking hours to their industry, then are they really what they say they are?

Keep asking the hard questions.